2021

New York

MANHATTAN

Restaurants

The Food Enthusiast's
Long Weekend Guide

Andrew Delaplaine

GET 3 FREE NOVELS
Like political thrillers?
See next page to download 3 FREE page-turning
novels—no strings attached.

Andrew Delaplaine is the Food Enthusiast.
When he's not playing tennis,
he dines anonymously
at the Publisher's expense.

WANT 3 *FREE* THRILLERS?

Why, of course you do!
If you like these writers--
Vince Flynn, Brad Thor, Tom Clancy, James Patterson,
David Baldacci, John Grisham, Brad Meltzer, Daniel
Silva, Don DeLillo
If you like these TV series –
House of Cards, Scandal, West Wing, The Good Wife,
Madam Secretary, Designated Survivor

You'll love the **unputdownable** series about
Jack Houston St. Clair, with political intrigue, romance,
and loads of action and suspense.

Besides writing travel books, I've written political thrillers
for many years that have delighted hundreds of thousands
of readers. I want to introduce you to my work!
Send me an email and I'll send you a link where you can
download the first 3 books in my bestselling series,
absolutely FREE.

Mention **this book** when you email me.

andrewdelaplaine@mac.com
Photo by Michael Discenza on Unsplash
Copyright © by Gramercy Park Press
All rights reserved.

MANHATTAN

The Food Enthusiast's Complete Restaurant Guide

Table of Contents

INTRODUCTION

There's a whole world of distinct neighborhoods in Manhattan. A whole wonderful world. Believe me, I have walked them all and enjoyed every minute of it (except when it was raining, and sometimes, even then).

For the purposes of this book, I am dividing the listings into 4 sections, Downtown, Midtown, Upper East Side and Upper West Side. But everybody knows there's much more to it than that.

EAST SIDE vs WEST SIDE
Fifth Avenue divides East from West. Anything east of Fifth Avenue is on the East Side; anything west is, well, you get it. The puzzling part assaults newcomers when they get down to 14th Street, where Downtown really begins. Here you get streets that are not numbered as much as named. Mott Street, Canal, Houston, Bleecker, etc. This gets very confusing.

AVENUE ADDRESSES
The great avenues of Manhattan are not as glamorous as the ones in Paris, but they are important because they are the main arteries that run north and south. The street address on an "avenue" means nothing to the outsider. You need to know the "cross street" to be able to locate it. That's why in the listings below,

you'll see something like "1234 Lexington Ave (bet. 30th and 31st Sts)," which tells you where it is without you having to pull out your cell phone and resort to Google Maps, which, by the way, you'll find extremely helpful.

MIDTOWN
Strictly speaking, Midtown runs from 34th Street to 59th Street, where Central Park begins. (For newbies, 59th Street is also called Central Park South.)

Downtown, most people agree, really starts at 14th Street. There's a great amount of wonderful activity going on between 14th Street and 34th Street, which is neither a part of Downtown, nor a part of Midtown. (I personally call it LoMi, for Lower Midtown, but nobody else does.)

In this book, however, I am including this "in between" area in the Midtown section. This includes neighborhoods like the Flower District, Hudson Yards, Kips Bay, NoMad, Chelsea, Gramercy Park (one of the many places I lived in New York), Union Square, the famous Meatpacking District, and others.

Midtown is divided between **Midtown West** and **Midtown East**, with, as I said above, Fifth Avenue being the dividing point.

DOWNTOWN

14th Street south. This takes many varied neighborhoods—Greenwich Village (East Village and West Village), Lower East Side, Nolita/NoLiTa, SoHo, Little Australia, Little Italy, Chinatown, the Financial District and a whole lot more. As noted above, I'm including LoMi in this section.

UPPER WEST SIDE

The Upper West Side really is Central Park West to the Hudson River, and from 59th Street up to 110th Street. When you hear the term "Upper Manhattan," it means the area north of 96th Street.

West Harlem runs from 125th Street to 155th Street. And it goes on and on.

UPPER EAST SIDE

Just as there is with the Upper West Side, the Upper East Side has several different neighborhoods. To a New Yorker, the Upper East Side means the area between 59th Street to 96th Street. East Harlem begins there and runs up to 141st Street, from Fifth Avenue east to the river. Within this is Yorkville (79th to 96th), Carnegie Hill (86th to 98th), and still others.

It's not as daunting as it sounds. But this is a BIG city, and it takes time to learn the many neighborhoods that make it up.

Chapter 1
DOWNTOWN

DID YOU FIND AN INTERESTING PLACE?
If you discover a place you think I should check out on my next visit, drop me a line, will you? I'll mention your name if I end up listing it.
andrewdelaplaine@mac.com

ANTON'S

570 Hudson St (bet. 11th St & Perry St), 212-924-0818

www.antonsnyc.com

CUISINE: American (Traditional) / Wine Bar / Italian

DRINKS: Full bar

SERVING: Dinner nightly; Lunch also Fri – Sun.

PRICE RANGE: $$$

NEIGHBORHOOD: West Village

A cozy little café and wine bar with a simple but very good menu. Old-school New York atmosphere, one of those places in the Village where it's just as welcoming whether you slip in for a lovely dinner in the little room, or drop in at the bar for a nightcap on your way home. This part of town has buildings that are human scale, so the whole neighborhood is very comfortable. The building dates from 1850. Some seating outside in good weather. Favorites: Chopped chicken liver & hearts (I love this dish, though a lot of people recoil at the very idea of it); Spinach Ravioli drizzled with sage butter; Pork Rib Chop (expertly grilled); and the Hanger Steak. Nice wine selection.

ATERA

77 Worth St. (Church St.), New York: 212-226-1444.

www.ateranyc.com

CUISINE: New American

DRINKS: Full bar; wine paring available.

SERVING: Tues-Sat only. Single seating at 6:30. Takes 3 hours. (Reserve 2 months out for weekend seating)

Prix fixe menu only, costing several hundred dollars per person if you get the wine parings. Only 13 chairs per night (plus a single table).
NEIGHBORHOOD: TriBeCa
PRICE RANGE: $$$$
You'll get whatever the chef wants to make the night you visit. (They "present" the menu to you, but only at the end of your visit.) With 20 or so courses, you won't be disappointed. You get to watch all this from your perch on a bar stool where you see them make the food with a reverence that almost seems to be too much. They put the plate in front of you and you wonder if you're supposed to bow to it or eat it. Eat it.

BABBO
110 Waverly Pl (bet. N Washington Sq & Mac Dougal St), 212-777-0303
www.babbonyc.com
CUISINE: Italian
DRINKS: Full Bar
SERVING: Dinner, Lunch (Tues – Sat)
PRICE RANGE: $$$$
NEIGHBORHOOD: Greenwich Village
High-end Italian eatery of Mario Batali's located in a repurposed carriage house. Great welcoming atmosphere. Menu favorites: Spicy two-minute Calamari; Barbecued skirt steak; Lamb chops. Extensive menu. Make reservations.

BALTHAZAR
80 Spring St (bet. Crosby St & Broadway), 212-965-1414
www.balthazarny.com

CUISINE: French
DRINKS: Full Bar
SERVING: Breakfast, Lunch & Dinner
PRICE RANGE: $$$
NEIGHBORHOOD: SoHo

Iconic French brasserie featuring classy interior and impressive menu and a winning crowd with lots of buzz about it. Bobby Flay says he likes the steak frites and coq au vin here. Another great chef, Eric Ripert, likes the steak frites, too, but says, "I go as often as I can—they have great energy, good service, and fantastic steak frites." Other Menu picks: French toast with bacon and Chicken Liver & Foie Gras Mousse. Great dining experience. A favorite for any meal.

BANTY ROOSTER
24 Greenwich Ave (bet. Charles St & 10th St), 646-767-9227
www.thebantynyc.com

CUISINE: American (New) / SW U.S. / Puerto Rican / some Asian
DRINKS: Full bar
SERVING: Dinner
PRICE RANGE: $$
NEIGHBORHOOD: West Village
Casual eatery with an interior that's bright (even at night), with whitewashed rough brick walls, a wooden ceiling that's also been painted over in white, sharp clean surfaces. Serves mainly upscale Southwestern fare, but there are accents from other parts of the world, with specialty items from as far away as Guam down to Puerto Rico. A small bar area is toward the rear. Menu picks: Fried chicken skin is a starter I like; Half chicken with rice and Short ribs; Pork Collar pan-roasted. Affordable wine offerings.

BAR BELLY (Formerly Lead Belly)
14B Orchard St (bet. Canal St & Hester St), 917-488-0943
www.barbellynyc.com
CUISINE: Seafood
DRINKS: Full Bar
SERVING: Dinner; closed Sundays
PRICE RANGE: $$
NEIGHBORHOOD: Chinatown, Lower East Side
Popular neighborhood eatery (almost no tourists) with a purposeful down market shabby look. Great seafood selection. Crowded on weekends. Happy hour specials (oysters and craft cocktails expertly rendered by the gifted bartenders). Live music and DJ.

BATARD

239 West Broadway (bet. Walker St & Beach St),
212-219-2777
www.batardtribeca.com
CUISINE: Modern European/American
(New)/French
DRINKS: Full Bar
SERVING: Dinner; Closed Sun
PRICE RANGE: $$$$
NEIGHBORHOOD: TriBeCa

Those of you with long memories will recognize that
Batard's location is more famous than it is, having
once housed such culinary stars as Corton and, going
back to 1985, Montrachet. This was where Daniel
Boulud got his start. This place has seen the
neighborhood change over the years, becoming what
might now be considered the most interesting part of
Manhattan to live or work in. Batard today is an
upscale eatery offering a creative menu of European,
American and French cuisine. One thing about it that
is so impressive is the quality of its food without the
pretentiousness found in so many other places. The
wine list is a wonderful example of the best quality
with fair prices. Lots of great selections from Alsace,
Austria, Germany, but a great selection of red and
white Burgundy. Favorites: Black bass with roasted
shrimp & fennel, Octopus is beautifully prepared, the
Duck exquisite. Braised pork shoulder with savoy
cabbage surprisingly lighter than it sounds. Great
presentation. Delicious desserts.

THE BEATRICE INN

285 W 12th St (bet. 4th St & 8th Ave), 212-675-2808

www.thebeatriceinn.com
CUISINE: American (Traditional)/Seafood
DRINKS: Full Bar
SERVING: Dinner; closed Mondays
PRICE RANGE: $$$
NEIGHBORHOOD: West Village
Vanity Fair editor Graydon Carter (or is it Carter Graydon?) opened this little upscale chophouse and the celebrities flocked. Great atmosphere, especially in the winter when the fireplace is lit. They touch all the bases, from the opening round of expertly created craft cocktails through to the stunning desserts. Favorites: Roast Duck flambé and Milk braised pork shoulder. Ideal for a very special celebration. Reservations recommended.

BRINDLE ROOM
277 E 10th St (bet. Ave A & 1st Ave), 212-529-9702
https://brindleroomny.com
CUISINE: American (New)
DRINKS: Beer & Wine Only
SERVING: Lunch & Dinner; Dinner only on Mondays
PRICE RANGE: $$
NEIGHBORHOOD: East Village, Alphabet City
Small, intimate gastropub offering a menu of American comfort food. Menu picks: Burger (one of the best in town because it contains a seasoned blend including dry-aged rib eye deckle) and Blackened Pork with Kale and zucchini gratin. Complimentary donut holes offered at end of meal. Happy hour specials. Reservations recommended.

BUBBY'S
120 Hudson St, 212-219-0666
www.bubbys.com
CUISINE: American
DRINKS: Full Bar
SERVING: Breakfast, Lunch, Dinner
PRICE RANGE: $$
NEIGHBORHOOD: Tribeca
Known for its traditional American cuisine, here everything is made from scratch using traditional family recipes. Menu favorites include: Pulled pork and Fried chicken – each order comes with the restaurant's signature buttermilk biscuits. For dessert there's a selection of home-baked pies and cakes.

BUDDAKAN
75 9th Ave (nr. W 16th St) 212-989-6699
www.buddakannyc.com
CUISINE: Chinese/Asian Fusion
DRINKS: Full Bar
SERVING: Dinner
PRICE RANGE: $$$
NEIGHBORHOOD: Meatpacking District, Chelsea
Of course, in Chinatown, you get the "most authentic" Chinese food, but this place in Chelsea comes mighty close to the best of the best if you're looking for authenticity. Large, lavishly decorated eatery offering an impressive menu of Asian fare. Favorites: Glazed Alaskan black cod and Monk fish. Creative cocktails. A luxurious dining experience.

CARBONE
181 Thompson St (bet. Houston St & Bleecker St),
212-254-3000
www.carbonenewyork.com
CUISINE: Italian
DRINKS: Full Bar
SERVING: Lunch & Dinner; Dinner only on Sat &
Sun
PRICE RANGE: $$$$
NEIGHBORHOOD: Greenwich Village
High-end Italian eatery that attracts the A-list crowd,
making it one of the toughest spots to secure a table.
(Don't order too much—portions are generous.) The
veal parmigiana is the size of a hubcap. This is one of
the few places where they make Caesar salad
tableside (remember when they used to do that
everywhere?), so you can always get more anchovies
right away without having to send the waiter back to
the kitchen later. Beautiful & fun dining experience.
When you first enter, it's tight and packed, but this
soon gives way to 3 dining rooms. Tourists arrive
early, and locals come in later, but the vibe at all
times is very welcoming. Menu picks: Burrata with
Eggplant caponata and Veal parmesan. Superior wine
list, with some 250 selections, about half Italian.
Book ahead.

CHARLIE BIRD
5 King St (nr. Houston St), with entrance on 6th
Avenue, 212-235-7133
www.charliebirdnyc.com
CUISINE: Italian
DRINKS: Full Bar

SERVING: Lunch & Dinner
PRICE RANGE: $$$
NEIGHBORHOOD: border of SoHo & West Village
This two-level eatery offers New American fare with
a heavy Italian twist. Fried squash blossoms stuffed
with cheese and anchovies are an amuse bouche;
Chicken liver; Cappellacci pasta topped with puree of
peas and guanciale; crispy-skinned chicken cooked
under a brick is delectable; and the Veal Chop.
Standout dessert is the molten chocolate cake. Nice
wine selection (tilted toward Italy) has about 120
selections, all quite good. About 40 of them are
priced under $100.

CHUMLEY'S
86 Bedford St, 212-675-2081
https://chumleysnewyork.com
CUISINE: American (New)
DRINKS: Full Bar
SERVING: Dinner; Closed Sun
PRICE RANGE: $$$
NEIGHBORHOOD: West Village
Legendary speakeasy updated with a sophisticated
menu of New American fare. Favorites: Pork Ribeye
and Duck Pie. Ring the bell at the door for entrance.
Speakeasy atmosphere with an onsite historian.
Reservations necessary.

CROSBY STREET BAR
79 Crosby St (bet. Prince & Spring Sts), 212-226-6400
www.firmdalehotels.com
CUISINE: American
DRINKS: Full Bar
SERVING: Breakfast, Lunch, Dinner
PRICE RANGE: $$$$
NEIGHBORHOOD: SoHo
Located on a quiet cobblestoned street in the **Crosby Street Hotel**, this bar, in addition to its funky British charm, features classic English afternoon tea. The menu is creative but the portions are small. The bar offers specialty cocktails and an international wine list. Outdoor seating available. (Be sure to slip into the bathroom for a look at the wallpaper.)

DISTILLED
211 W Broadway (at Franklin St), 646-809-9490

www.distillednn.com

CUISINE: American (with many twists)
DRINKS: Full bar; creative cocktails
SERVING: Dinner nightly; brunch on weekends
NEIGHBORHOOD: TriBeCa
PRICE RANGE: $$

The wide round wheel-like chandeliers hanging from the very high ceiling in here make you gasp for a second when you walk in. I remember seeing similar gargoyle-type wagon wheels in steakhouses in my youth. But these are fun.

The dark woods and cozy booths give off a warm feeling, and so does the staff.

Lots of whimsical twists on classic pub fare: chicken wings, yes, but amped up with gochujang and chili paste; a BLT, yes, but with sunflower sprouts, slivers of bacon, basil and tomatoes on sourdough; onion rings, yes, but fried, frozen and then fried again.

The burger is made with grass-fed beef, but my favorite is the duck they treat like chicken: it's breaded and fried. (I can honestly say I've never had it prepared so simply. I thought it would be dry, but it was succulent.)

A lot of other little twists and turns on the menu, but all of them exciting and unexpected. A fun place you'll love.

ESTELA
47 E Houston St (bet. Greene St & Mulberry St), 212-219-7693
www.estelanyc.com
CUISINE: American (New)

DRINKS: Full Bar
SERVING: Dinner; Lunch Fri - Sun
PRICE RANGE: $$$
NEIGHBORHOOD: Nolita, NoHo
Popular eatery serving small plates of American fare with a Mediterranean twist. Favorites: Beef tartare with sunchoke and Grilled foie gras and grape leaf. Intimate dining experience. Nice wine selection.

ESSEX MARKET
88 Essex St (Cor. Essex & Delancey Sts), no phone
https://www.essexmarket.nyc/
CUISINE: Food Court
DRINKS: Full bar
SERVING: 7 a.m. – 1 a.m.

PRICE RANGE: $$-$$$
NEIGHBORHOOD: Lower East Side
This is an historic market, opened originally in 1940 to house many of the vendors that had pushcarts along the crowded streets of the Lower East Side. They've had to move into different buildings over the years, and this is the newest, so you'd never know the history of the Market by just walking in here. There's a 90-minute walking & tasting tour Tuesday night and Saturday morning, from Turnstile Tours, https://turnstiletours.com/ I took it one rainy afternoon and it was a lot of fun. Essex has lots of vendors offering nearly everything. GROCERY (Luna Brothers Fruit, Luis Meat Market, etc.); SPECIALTY (Formaggio Essex, Olive & Spice, Tops Hops, Café d'Avignon (bakery), Japanese Deli & more; PREPARED FOODS (such as Arancini Brothers, offering Sicilian street food, Puebla Mexican Food, Dominican Cravings, Don Ceviche, Mille Nonne offering Italian cuisine, Zerza, with Moroccan food, etc.). Downstairs you'll find the **MARKET LINE**, which has another batch of vendors offering even more. www.marketline.nyc You can see how real New Yorkers live and shop when you visit a place like this.

FAIRFAX
234 W 4th St (bet. 10th St & Charles St), 212-933-1824
www.fairfax.nyc
CUISINE: Café/Wine Bar
DRINKS: Full Bar
SERVING: Breakfast, Lunch, & Dinner

PRICE RANGE: $$$
NEIGHBORHOOD: West Village
This all-day café (part coffee shop/part wine bar)
offers a menu of Mediterranean small plates. There's
a well-worn leather sofa in the corner with a couple of
huge chunks of marble in front of it where I like to
relax with drinks. Favorites: Soft poached eggs and
soldiers (strips of cheesy bread) and Carbonara
Flatbread. The omelets are cooked in the French
style—light, fluffy, perfect. Great choice for brunch.

FEAST
102 Third Ave. (at 13th St.), 212-529-8880
www.eatfeastnyc.com
CUISINE: New American
DRINKS: Beer & wine only
SERVING: Opens from 8-4 weekdays for coffee and
pastries baked on premise; dinner nightly from 6

(except Sun, when they serve brunch from 11-4, but are closed for dinner)
NEIGHBORHOOD: Lower East Side / East Village
PRICE RANGE: $$

The rough brick walls, the narrow room, the basket of fruit on the bar—it's all very cozy here at Feast, where locals congregate for Chef Christopher Meenan's simple yet evocative family-style food with seasonal menus with ingredients drawn from area farms and purveyors. The idea is that you get to choose a certain type of "feast" and the menu is built around that. Example: the Farmer's Market Feast would be all veggies, summer succotash, stuffed eggplant, zucchini 3 ways, etc. The Pork Feast would include courses starting with house-made charcuterie, BBQ pulled pork, pork Milanese, pig's ear taco, things like that. All very inventive. (I don't know why they call it "family-style": my mom never made me lemon souffle pancakes with mixed-berry coulis.)

GATO
324 Lafayette St (bet. Houston St & Bleecker St), 212-334-6400
www.gatonyc.com
CUISINE: Mediterranean/Spanish
DRINKS: Full Bar
SERVING: Dinner
PRICE RANGE: $$$
NEIGHBORHOOD: NoHo

Hip eatery (one of Bobby Flay's) in a huge ballroom-sized location. Flay is actually from New York, so this is yet another homecoming. This incarnation of Flay's is like a cross between his shuttered Mesa Grill and his Bolo spot. While the menu here is described as "New Mediterranean," it's more influenced by Spain than any other cuisine. The huge bar is always packed three-deep it seems, but the bar is the place to be to enjoy the bite-sized plates and tapas dishes. The simple wooden tables and café-style cane chairs throw off a casual vibe. The music cranks up the later the evening gets, which is why I prefer to go a little early. The colorful brick walls and floor tiles make the sound seem much louder. Favorites: Ricotta & plum crostini; artichoke and wild mushroom paella; mussel & clam salad; chorizo crépinette; I particularly liked the white anchovies topped with a dollop of sour orange sauce; squid rings with bacon bits sprinkled on top also are very good. Nice dessert selection.

GOTHAM BAR & GRILL

12 E 12th St (bet. 5th Ave & University Pl), 212-620-4020
www.gothambarandgrill.com
CUISINE: American (New)
DRINKS: Full Bar
SERVING: Lunch, & Dinner, Dinner only on Sat & Sun
PRICE RANGE: $$$$
NEIGHBORHOOD: Union Square/Greenwich Village

A romantic fixture (for over 3 decades) offering a menu of New American classics in a big open room on a quiet Village street. You can look down into the dining room from a big long bar on the left side of the room that's raised a couple of steps. The lampshades that look like parachutes cast a lovely glow while jazz quietly plays in the background. Favorites: Roast Niman Ranch Pork and Soft-Shell Crabs. Try the key-lime pie served with ice cream.

GREEN GARDEN VILLAGE
216 Grand St (bet. Mott St & Elizabeth St), 646-912-9136
No Website
CUISINE: Dim Sum/Noodles/ Cantonese
DRINKS: No Booze
SERVING: Breakfast, Lunch, Dinner
PRICE RANGE: $$
NEIGHBORHOOD: Little Italy
The Duck is their specialty but their menu impresses. Favorites: BBQ Pork and Alaskan King Crab. Most dishes served family style. Great atmosphere – like an old style Chinatown eatery.

HARRY'S CAFÉ & STEAK
1 Hanover Sq (bet. William St & Stone St), 212-785-9200
www.harrysnyc.com
CUISINE: Steakhouse
DRINKS: Full Bar
SERVING: Lunch, & Dinner; Closed Sun
PRICE RANGE: $$$
NEIGHBORHOOD: Financial District
Popular and very comfortable steakhouse with an adjoining café. Harry's has been around for decades and it remains a wonderful place prized by first-timers and the hundreds of locals that come here regularly. Lots of nooks and crannies as well as

platforms which are great for people-watching. Solid food, great portions, perfect to satisfy a hearty appetite. The menu has changed a little to reflect the shift in population in the area, so now besides the typical NYC steakhouse fare, you can get things like seafood tacos. But don't. This place has been known for its wonderful steaks, its raw bar and its Caesar salad, so get a steak, like the 20-oz bone-in strip, a 16-oz Cajun rib eye, a prime hanger steak. French onion soup is great.

HIGH STREET ON HUDSON
637 Hudson St (bet. Gansevoort St & Horatio St), 917-388-3944
www.highstreetonhudson.com
CUISINE: American (New)
DRINKS: Full Bar
SERVING: Breakfast, Lunch, & Dinner
PRICE RANGE: $$
NEIGHBORHOOD: West Village
Popular Philly spin-off eatery offering a menu of seasonal American cuisine. This is one of those places where you wish you lived on the same block, because you'd enjoy it whether you came here for breakfast, lunch or dinner. If you did live on the same block, you'd be here several times a week, different times of the day. The in-house bakery accounts for the delicious breads and pastries. For b'fast, get the Hickory Town sandwich with Lancaster bologna, fried egg and pickled mayo. At lunch, try the duck meatball sub. For dinner, try the honey-glazed chicken with the chicken skin Caesar salad. Or grilled fish.

I SODI
105 Christopher St (bet. Bedford St & Bleecker St),
212-414-5774
www.isodinyc.com
CUISINE: Tuscan
DRINKS: Full Bar
SERVING: Dinner
PRICE RANGE: $$$
NEIGHBORHOOD: West Village
Intimate, romantic eatery (only 8 or 9 tables and some
bar stools) with a long bar on one side and tables on
the other. Food is firmly rooted in Tuscany. Don't
expect dishes from any other part of Italy, which
makes this place so damned wonderful—it is what it
is, and what it is is perfect. The pastas here are top-
notch and the portions are large. I like the tortelli
made with chestnut flour and stuffed with chestnuts
or the ravioli filled with ricotta & spinach. Tagliata
(grilled sirloin) is excellent; the Cornish game hen
cooked under a cast iron weight is sublime, with the
thinnest possible breading giving a crackle to the skin
when you bite into it; the lasagna will melt in your
mouth. Wine list is a trifle high-priced.

IL BUCO ALIMENTARI E VINERIA

53 Great Jones St. (bet. Bowery & Lafayette St.),
New York: 212-837-2622.
www.ilbucovineria.com
CUISINE: Italian
DRINKS: Beer & wine
SERVING: Lunch, dinner
NEIGHBORHOOD: NoHo
PRICE RANGE: $$-$$$

The copper, the imported tiles from Italy, the communal tables of wood all combine to make you feel like you're in the Old Country. The Market in the front offers all kinds of artisanal things for sale, but it's the aromas escaping from the open kitchen in the back (redolent with some from wood they use to cook with) is what you'll want to focus on. Seasonal menu, so it changes, but expect things like short ribs, rabbit fried and sauced, crispy polenta, porchetta alla Romana. Donna Leonard, who has **Il Buco** over at 47 Bond St., set this place up.

KATZ'S DELICATESSEN
205 E. Houston St. (at Ludlow St.), 212-254-2246
www.katzsdelicatessen.com
CUISINE: Deli, Sandwiches
DRINKS: Beer & Wine
SERVING: Breakfast, Lunch, Dinner
NEIGHBORHOOD: Lower East Side
PRICE RANGE: $$
Of course, there's nothing quite like Katz's Deli
anywhere. If you want to have a corned beef or
pastrami sandwich in New York, have it here. (The
knoblewurst with its pungent garlic and fat is also an
excellent choice, but so are the potato latkes.) You
think you've been in a Jewish Deli—you haven't till
you've been here. Also excellent because of the
colorful clientele. Open since 1888. $$

L'ATELIER DE JOEL ROBUCHON
85 Tenth Ave (bet. Ave of the Americas & 5th Ave),
212-488-8885
www.joelrobuchonusa.com
CUISINE: French
DRINKS: Full Bar
SERVING: Dinner; Closed Sun & Mon
PRICE RANGE: $$$$
NEIGHBORHOOD: Meatpacking District, Chelsea
Wildly expensive upscale eatery with a big U-shaped
dining counter that looks onto the kitchen. You sit on
red leather stools. There are a few tables against the
wall for bigger groups. Fine modern French cuisine
and tasting menus. Favorites: Wagyu beef, King crab
in avocado cannelloni, Veal sweetbreads; Veal cheeks
confit "blanquette-style"; and Sliders crowned with a

dab of foie gras. Beautiful spot for romantic or special occasions. Finish things off with an excellent chocolate soufflé.

LAFAYETTE GRAND CAFÉ & BAKERY
380 Lafayette St (bet. 4th St & Great Jones St), 212-533-3000
www.lafayetteny.com
CUISINE: French/Bakery
DRINKS: Full Bar
SERVING: Breakfast, Lunch & Dinner
PRICE RANGE: $$$
NEIGHBORHOOD: NoHo
Belle Epoque-style brasserie/bakery combination serving classic French fare: beef tartare with watercress & a quail egg; delicate butter lettuce with Roquefort, country ham and a tangy herb vinaigrette; one of the best steak frites in town. The impressive selection of bakery confections make it a favorite for breakfast as well. Delicious pastas.

LOCANDA VERDE
Greenwich Hotel
377 Greenwich St. (at N. Moore St.), New York: 212-925-3797
www.locandaverdenyc.com
CUISINE: Italian, American
DRINKS: Full bar
SERVING: Lunch, Dinner

NEIGHBORHOOD: TriBeCa
PRICE RANGE: $$$
Robert De Niro is partnered with star **Chef Andrew Carmellini** to bring you this hip trendy spot. Casual comfort food exceedingly good: go for a pasta dish unless you're there when they offer fried chicken. Chocolate donuts for dessert a must.

MARKET LINE
115 Delancey St (corner Norfolk St & Delancey St) – no phone; individual vendors have phones
www.marketline.nyc
CUISINE: Food Court
DRINKS: Full bar
SERVING: 7 a.m. – 1 a.m.
PRICE RANGE: $$
NEIGHBORHOOD: Lower East Side
Located downstairs from the **ESSEX MARKET**, this food collection offers 30 locally-sourced vendors and restaurants. Some of the eateries include: Ukrainian Diner & Grocer Veselka, family-run German butcher

shop and grocer founded in 1937 Schaller & Weber, and 1920s tea parlor and dim sum eatery Nom Wah. Seating in the middle, some of the larger places have their own dining space.

MIMI
185 Sullivan St (bet. Houston St & Bleecker St), 212-418-1260
www.miminyc.com
CUISINE: French
DRINKS: Full Bar
SERVING: Dinner, Lunch only on Sat & Sun
PRICE RANGE: $$$
NEIGHBORHOOD: West Village
Contemporary eatery offering a menu of elaborate French classics (with some modern twists) in a very small bistro on a quiet street in the Village. Favorites: Chicken liver mousse, pot-au-feu (with tuna), Rabbit ballotine with sweet peaches, Sweetbreads with lobster mushrooms, Veal tartare and Clams with Squid. Don't leave without trying the Espresso Martini.

MOMOFUKU MILK BAR
251 E 13th St (near Second Ave), 646-692-4154
www.milkbarstore.com
CUISINE: Bakery, Ice Cream & Frozen Yogurt
DRINKS: No Booze
SERVING: Desserts
PRICE RANGE: $$
NEIGHBORHOOD: East Village
This dessert specialty shop offers a variety of freshly baked cookies, cakes and pies. Popular items include

the Confetti Cookie and Cornflake Baking Mixes.
Specialty favorites include Cereal Milk (milk that
tastes like it was poured from a bowl of cereal). Small
lunch menu available. Novelty items for sale like T-
shirts, bags, and cookbooks.

MOMOFUKU SSÄM BAR
207 Second Ave (at 13th St.), 212-254-3500
www.momofuku.com/new-york/ssam-bar/
CUISINE: Korean, American
DRINKS: Full bar
SERVING: Lunch, Dinner
NEIGHBORHOOD: East Village
PRICE RANGE: $$$
Pork buns, pork buns, pork buns. Braised goat also a
winner. Smart crowd here, loud and bustling. Loads
of fun. There's that special excitement that is New
York in this place.

MIGHTY QUINN'S BARBECUE
103 Second Av. (nr. 6th St.), 212-677-3733
www.mightyquinnsbbq.com
CUISINE: BBQ / Southern
DRINKS: Beer & Wine
SERVING: Lunch, Dinner
NEIGHBORHOOD: East Village
PRICE RANGE: $
Sustainable smoked meats. They started with a little
street side stand and now have a roof over their heads.
Get the sweet potato casserole with maple syrup and
pecans.

MISSION CHINESE FOOD
171 E Broadway, New York: 917-376-5660
www.missionchinesefood.com
CUISINE: Chinese
DRINKS: Full bar
SERVING: Lunch, Fri-Tues, 12-3; dinner, Thurs-
Tues, from 5:30. Reserve on missionresy@gmail.com
NEIGHBORHOOD: Lower East Side
PRICE RANGE: $$
Chef Danny Bowien started in San Francisco, but
he's made quite a splash here, wowing all the critics
and attracting a sophisticated crowd to this little joint.
Salt cod fried rice, beef brisket, cumin lamb breast,
catfish.

MORANDI
211 Waverly Pl (bet. Charles St & 10th St), 212-627-
7575
www.morandiny.com
CUISINE: Italian

DRINKS: Full Bar
SERVING: Breakfast, Lunch & Dinner
PRICE RANGE: $$$
NEIGHBORHOOD: West Village
Rustic trattoria serving an impressive menu of Italian cuisine that attracts Chef Bobby Flay more than any other eatery in town. Menu picks: Gnocchi with pancetta and Tagliatelle Bolognese. Impressive wine and cocktail selection. Sidewalk seating.

MOTORINO
349 E 12th St (bet. 1st Ave & 2nd Ave), 212-777-2644
www.motorinopizza.com
CUISINE: Pizza/Italian
DRINKS: Beer & Wine Only
SERVING: Lunch & Dinner
PRICE RANGE: $$
NEIGHBORHOOD: East Village
Small eatery serving great pizza (also delivers) and Italian fare. The pizza here is Neapolitan in style and his big blistered crusts. Usually a wait as it's always busy.

NAMI NORI
33 Carmine St (bet. Ave of the Americas & Bedford St), 646-998-4588
www.naminori.nyc
CUISINE: Japanese / Temaki Bar
DRINKS: Beer & Wine
SERVING: Lunch & Dinner, Dinner only on Sat; Closed Sundays
PRICE RANGE: $$
NEIGHBORHOOD: West Village
In a light and airy room, you'll find this minimalist hand-roll eatery offering an impressive selection. Favorites: Spicy crab Dynamite and Lobster tempura. You must try the furikaké fries with tomato tonkatsu.

Vegetarian options. So simple, basic, cheerful … very well done. Mostly bar seating but turn-around is fast.

NARCISSA
25 Cooper Sq (bet. Bowery & 4th St), 212-228-3344
www.narcissarestaurant.com
CUISINE: American (New)
DRINKS: Full Bar
SERVING: Dinner, Lunch on Sat & Sun
PRICE RANGE: $$$
NEIGHBORHOOD: East Village
Next to the Standard Hotel is this popular upscale eatery offering a menu of refined, farm-to-table New American cuisine. The succulent baby chickens from the rotisserie are famous. Two dining rooms and an open kitchen. Private garden open weather permitting. Limited wine selection. Reservations recommended.

NOWON
507 E 6th St (bet. Ave B & Ave A), 646-692-3867

www.nowonnyc.com
CUISINE: Korean/American (New)
DRINKS: Beer & Wine
SERVING: Dinner
PRICE RANGE: $$
NEIGHBORHOOD: East Village, Alphabet City
Small eatery serving interesting combos that must be tried to believe. Favorites: Honey Butter tater tots; Octopus & Spam Fried Rice; Sizzling Kimchi Rice.

PORTALE
126 W 18th St (bet. 7th Ave & Ave of the Americas), 917-781-0255
www.portalerestaurant.com
CUISINE: Italian
DRINKS: Full bar
SERVING: Dinner
PRICE RANGE: $$$
NEIGHBORHOOD: Chelsea
Comfortable eatery offering Italian/American fare in a very cozy room with distressed wooden planks painted white lining one wall. The place was filled with a fun, busy crowd when I came in with a friend to escape a nasty winter night. Favorites: Foie Gras Tortellini; Mushroom Risotto. Try the Meatball Sliders and you'll be hooked. Delicious gelati for dessert. Nice bar scene.

RAOUL'S
180 Prince St (near Sullivan St), 212-966-3518
www.raouls.com
CUISINE: French
DRINKS: Full Bar

SERVING: Dinner
PRICE RANGE: $$$
NEIGHBORHOOD: South Village
This intimate neighborhood gem offers a nice menu
with tasty authentic French bistro dishes like steak
frites (their signature dish). Delicious desserts like
crème brûlée.

RIDDLER
51 Bank St (bet. Waverly Pl & 4th St), 212-741-5136
www.theriddlerbar.com
CUISINE: Champagne Bar / Oysters / Burgers
DRINKS: Beer & Wine Only
SERVING: Dinner
PRICE RANGE: $$$
NEIGHBORHOOD: West Village
Small and very elegant Champagne bar boasting over
150 Champagnes by the bottle. Menu includes mostly
light bites like oysters, burgers, with a few entrees
like seared halibut – French-inspired comfort food.

The focus is the Champagne—nice selection of wines by the glass, both sparkling and still.

ROSEMARY'S
18 Greenwich Av., New York: 212-647-1818
http://rosemarysnyc.com/
CUISINE: Italian
DRINKS: Beer & Wine
SERVING: Breakfast, Lunch, Dinner, Brunch; no reservations except for parties of 8+.
NEIGHBORHOOD: Greenwich Village
PRICE RANGE: $$
Named after the boss's mother, this place maintains a garden on the rooftop of the building. Homemade pastas. A cute little place. Wine list has $40 bottles; by the glass for $10. Lamb, porchettina, braised pork shoulder.

RUSS AND DAUGHTERS
179 E Houston St (bet. E Houston St & 2nd Ave),
212-475-4880
www.russanddaughters.com
CUISINE: Smokehouse
DRINKS: No Booze
SERVING: Breakfast, Lunch, & Dinner
PRICE RANGE: $$
NEIGHBORHOOD: Lower East Side
A NYC institution since 1914 (and still owned by the
same family) serving quality smoked fish, homemade
pickled lox, traditional baked goods, smoked
sturgeon, whole smoked trout, herring, whitefish and
other specialty foods. Their bagels are famous. You
walk in here and the first thing you do is grab a
number by the door and with for it to be called. The
wait is always worth it. You can taste anything they
have before you order it. There aren't many stores
like this left in New York. (They were called
"appetizing" stores because they were formed based
on Kosher rules—if you wanted meat, you went to a
delicatessen; if you wanted fish or cream cheese or
bagels, you went to an "appetizing" store.)

SOHO DINER
Soho Grand Hotel
320 W Broadway (bet. Canal St & Grand St) 212-
965-3011
www.sohodinernyc.com
CUISINE: Diner
DRINKS: Full Bar
SERVING: Open 24 hours
PRICE RANGE: $$

NEIGHBORHOOD: South Village, TriBeCa
Diner atmosphere in the Soho Grand Hotel serving
"elevated diner fare," which means it costs a little
more than a regular diner (but not really). The
portions are substantial. And the place is clean as a

whistle. Since it's open 24 hours, I stumble-bumble
my way in here if I'm in this part of town late at night
and have had too much to drink (this happens
occasionally)—I always get the same thing, the Egg
Sandwich, with 2 eggs on a Kaiser roll with tomato
aioli. (The bacon is extra, but get it—it really makes
this sandwich stand out.) Then off to bed. It's good,
it's quick, it's cheap. Menu picks: Rigatoni
Bolognese; and Ham Steak & Eggs with chimichurri.
Large menu (75 items) but no substitutions. Cocktails
and old-school sodas. Jukebox plays vinyl.

THE SMILE

26 Bond St (near Lafayette St), 646-329-5836
www.thesmilenyc.com
CUISINE: American
DRINKS: Full Bar
SERVING: Lunch, Dinner, Brunch
PRICE RANGE: $$
NEIGHBORHOOD: NoHo / Washington Square
Popular among the young, artsy crowd, this coffee
shop style restaurant offers a rustic yet friendly
atmosphere just east of Washington Square. Menu
favorites include: Egg-ham-Gruyère-and-
caramelized-onion sandwich and Baked eggs with
tomato, Manchego, and avocado. Wine list, mostly
French, is small but moderately priced.

TEMPLE COURT

The Beekman Hotel
5 Beekman St (bet. Nassau St & Theatre Aly), 212-
658-1848
www.templecourtnyc.com
CUISINE: Steakhouse/Gastropub
DRINKS: Full Bar
SERVING: Breakfast, Lunch, & Dinner
PRICE RANGE: $$$
NEIGHBORHOOD: Financial District
Located in the landmark Beekman hotel, south of the
Brooklyn Bridge on-ramp, is this American restaurant
offering an impressive menu. The restaurant takes its
name from the building, which was called Temple
Court, built in 1881, before it became the Beekman.
The bar is a great experience, in a large open room
with an atrium that rises 9 floors. The dining room is

very luxe, with ornate embellishments, rich with leather, stained glass, deep polished woods, glittering chandeliers. Favorites: Duck a l'orange with baby fennel and Agnolotti, Monkfish with a hint of wood smoke, Spanish prawns with heads on, set off with roasted mushrooms and greens, Loin of lamb enhanced with lemon confit. The wine list is suitably impressive, but way overpriced. I drank Scotch the last time I was there, saving my party a good $300 to $500 by skipping the wine. Great desserts.

TETSU
78 Leonard St (bet. Broadway & Church St), 212-207-2370
www.tetsunyc.com
CUISINE: Japanese/Sushi
DRINKS: Full Bar
SERVING: Breakfast, Lunch, & Dinner
PRICE RANGE: $$
NEIGHBORHOOD: Tribeca/Civic Center
Popular eatery serving up raw, fried and robata-grilled Japanese dishes. Favorites: Bay scallops with asparagus and Chicken Yakitori. Creative cocktails. Get the "olive oil cake" for dessert. You've never had anything like it—yuzu flavored mascarpone cream, fresh thyme, orange zest, fleur de sel, yuzu sake, lemon zest, buttermilk.

TRIBECA GRILL
375 Greenwich St. (at Franklin St.), New York: 212-941-3900
www.myriadrestaurantgroup.com
CUISINE: American
DRINKS: Full bar
SERVING: Lunch, Dinner
NEIGHBORHOOD: TriBeCa
PRICE RANGE: $$$
They've developed a wildly supportive and sophisticated following. Maine lobster salad makes a good starter; Long Island duck breast, pan-roasted pork chop. Busy and fun bar scene.

WALLSÉ
344 W. 11th St. (at Washington St.), New York: 212-352-2300
www.kurtgutenbrunner.com/restaurants/wallse/
CUISINE: Austrian
DRINKS: Full bar
SERVING: Dinner nightly; Brunch on Sunday.
NEIGHBORHOOD: West Village
PRICE RANGE: $$$
Poached Maine Lobster with Quark Spaetzle; Viennese beef (sometimes oxtail) Goulash with sour cream; beef strip loin with crispy onions; lobster ravioli. In a perfectly wonderful setting that you think of when you think of Old New York: a tree-lined cobblestoned street.

WAVERLY INN
16 Bank St (bet. Waverly Pl & 4th St), 917-828-1154
www.waverlynyc.com

CUISINE: Steakhouse/Gastropub
DRINKS: Full Bar
SERVING: Breakfast, Lunch, & Dinner
PRICE RANGE: $$$
NEIGHBORHOOD: West Village
Upscale eatery offering a creative menu of American
comfort fare, steaks and oysters. Don't let the hype
scare you away. (The hype is getting a little tired
anyway.) Just because it's owned by former "Vanity
Fair" editor Graydon Carter and has the image of a
place where celebrities rule, people like you and me
really *can* get a table here. Cocktails served in a
clubby atmosphere on a quiet residential street in the
Village. This is one of those quintessentially New
York restaurants that I love so much, because it's
loud, boisterous and everybody seems to be having
such a good time. The leather banquettes, the low
lighting, the pictures of famous guests. In the
bathroom there are paintings of zebras and George
Gershwin at the piano smoking a cigar. Try the Black
Truffle Mac & Cheese, the Filet steak Diane, Jonah
crabcakes with more crab than breading, an excellent
burger. Almost like a downtown Joe Allen. Nice
choice for date night.

WOLFGANG'S STEAKHOUSE
409 Greenwich St (bet. Beach St & Hubert St), 212-
925-0350
www.wolfgangssteakhouse.net
CUISINE: Steakhouse
DRINKS: Full Bar
SERVING: Lunch & Dinner
PRICE RANGE: $$$$

NEIGHBORHOOD: Tribeca
Elegant high-end steakhouse tht has an "old New York" atmosphere you'll revel in. My favorite: the exquisite Porterhouse steak. Nice selection of wines. Seafood and vegetarian options available.

ZZ'S CLAM BAR
169 Thompson St (bet. Houston St & Bleecker St), 212-254-3000
www.zzsclambar.com
CUISINE: Seafood
DRINKS: Full Bar
SERVING: Dinner; closed Sunday & Monday
PRICE RANGE: $$$$
NEIGHBORHOOD: Greenwich Village
Hip, hot spot serving an impressive menu of seafood and raw bar specialties. Favorites: Tuna carpaccio with foie gras and Apple cocktail with shiso and basil. Raw oysters are perfection. Reservations only.

Downtown
Budget Spots

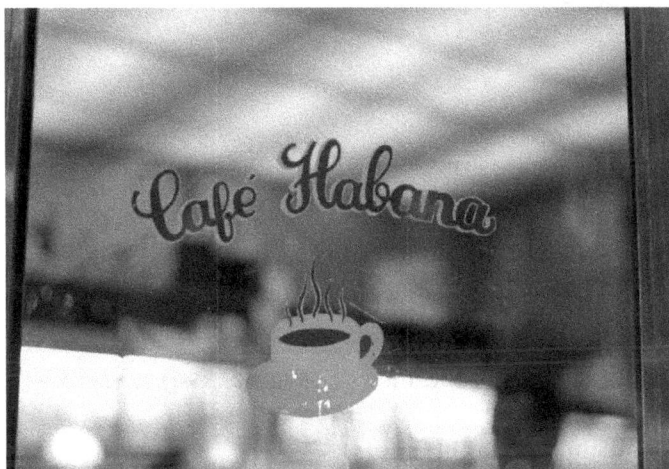

CAFÉ HABANA
17 Prince St (at Elizabeth St), New York: 212-625-2001
www.cafehabana.com/
CUISINE: Cuban, Mexican
DRINKS: Full bar
SERVING: Lunch, Dinner
NEIGHBORHOOD: NoLita
PRICE RANGE: $$
Hip little eatery with great food inspired by the Café Habana in Mexico City, not Havana. Tortas or burritos: Eggs with chorizo, grilled steak, Sloppy Joe BBQ pork sandwich, chicken Diablo, great soups.

The Cuban sandwich here was voted best in New York.

DUCKS EATERY
351 E. 12th St. (bet. First & Second Ave), 212-432-3825
www.duckseatery.com
CUISINE: BBQ (but much more)
DRINKS: Full bar
SERVING: Lunch (verify before going), dinner; brunch
NEIGHBORHOOD: East Village
PRICE RANGE: $$
Yes, they do have duck confit in this simple and charming little place, but I get the 6 sliders—little burgers with fried shallots. Under $10.

EMPELLON AL PASTOR
132 St Marks Pl (bet. Avenue A & 1st Ave), 646-833-7039
www.empellon.com

CUISINE: Mexican
DRINKS: Full Bar
SERVING: Breakfast, Lunch, & Dinner
PRICE RANGE: $
NEIGHBORHOOD: East Village
Offshoot of Empellón, this sister eatery offers a cheap
taco-focused menu that happens to be very good
indeed. Order from the counter at the far end of the
busy bar. Favorites: Breakfast burrito (served only at
dinner, oddly enough), Baby Back Rib Carnitas and
Chicken Nuggets. Tasty margaritas.

HANOI HOUSE
119 Saint Marks Pl, 212-995-5010
 www.hanoihousenyc.com
CUISINE: Vietnamese
DRINKS: Beer & Wine Only
SERVING: Dinner nightly, Lunch only on Sat
PRICE RANGE: $$
NEIGHBORHOOD: East Village, Alphabet City
Comfortable eatery offering a limited menu of
Vietnamese fare. Favorites: Spicy Octopus, Bun cha
with meatballs slightly charred wrapped in betel
leaves, Bo luc lac (filet mignon with honey, soy &
butter), Crispy Spring Rolls so good you could eat a
dozen of them.

NUM PANG SANDWICH SHOP
28 E 12 St, 646-791-0439
www.numpangnyc.com
CUISINE: Cambodian, Sandwiches
DRINKS: No Booze
SERVING: Lunch, Dinner

PRICE RANGE: $
NEIGHBORHOOD: Greenwich Village
This little shop is very small but VERY special, sandwiches with a Cambodian flair you'll remember forever. Menu favorites include: Pulled Pork and the 5 Spice Pork Belly sandwich.

SONS OF THUNDER
225 Pearl St, 646-822-0208
https://www.sonsofthunder.com/
CUISINE: Hot Dogs/Poke
DRINKS: Full Bar
SERVING: Lunch & Dinner; Closed Sunday
PRICE RANGE: $$
NEIGHBORHOOD: Financial District
Casual eatery specializing in Hawaiian and Californian flavors. Favorites: Huli Huli Teriyaki Chicken and Salmon poke bowl. Happy Hour. The 'Times' called this "the best poke in New York." And it's cheap!

Chapter 2
MIDTOWN
East & West

DID YOU FIND AN INTERESTING PLACE?
If you discover a place you think I should check out on my next visit, drop me a line, will you? I'll mention your name if I end up listing it.
andrewdelaplaine@mac.com

15 EAST
15 E 15th St, 212-647-0015
www.15eastrestaurant.com
CUISINE: Japanese, Sushi
DRINKS: Full bar
SERVING: Lunch, Dinner (except Sun., when closed)
NEIGHBORHOOD: Union Square, Flatiron
PRICE RANGE: $$$$
Chef Masato Shimizu oversees this sushi bar offering some of the best sushi in the city. Raves continue for this place. Why the sake is better here than anywhere else I'll never understand. (I hate sake, but all my friends insist this is the case here.)

21 CLUB
21 W 52nd St (near Fifth Ave), 212-582-7200
www.21club.com
CUISINE: American
DRINKS: Full bar
SERVING: Lunch, Dinner
NEIGHBORHOOD: Midtown West
PRICE RANGE: $$$$; no jeans, men must wear jacket.
You've got to experience this former speakeasy. The food's not as stellar as it was, but nobody comes here for the food. (Get the chicken hash, unique here.) They do enforce the dress code, although you don't have to wear a tie anymore. I was here once with my sister and brother-in-law meeting a guy, Peter Planes, and he showed up wearing jeans. Instead of going

home, he wanted to lunch here so bad that he went around the corner and bought a cheap pair of pants!

ABC KITCHEN
35 E 18th St (bet. Broadway & Park Ave S), 212-475-5829
www.abchome.com/eat/abc-kitchen
CUISINE: American, French
DRINKS: Full bar
SERVING: lunch weekdays, dinner nightly, brunch on weekends from 11.
NEIGHBORHOOD: Midtown South
PRICE RANGE: $$$

They're very conscious about their organic offerings here, which is highly unusual for a place that really cares about sustainable foods that also attracts a high-powered (and very stylish) crowd. The chef picks up produce from the nearby Union Square Greenmarket. Cheerful setting in a bright clean spot with old rustic beams saved from a crumbling barn that give the place some "texture." Pasta with greens, poached egg and lemon crumbs, calamari (the breading is crushed pretzels), ricotta cavatelli with shrimp and tomatoes. Whole wheat wood-fired pizzas are a specialty here: tomato, mozzarella, basil; or the fennel sausage, tomato, broccoli; or the clams, mint, parsley. Roast suckling pig with braised turnips a consistent winner.

AI FIORI
Langham Hotel
400 Fifth Ave (bet. 37th St & 36th St) 212-613-8660
www.aifiorinyc.com
CUISINE: Italian/French
DRINKS: Full Bar
SERVING: Breakfast, Lunch, & Dinner
PRICE RANGE: $$$$
NEIGHBORHOOD: Midtown East
Upscale eatery offering gourmet fare from the Italian and French Riviera, combining Italian ingredients with French technical mastery. Food, while rich, is not "heavy" in the way things used to be. Favorites: Braised Lamb; Veal-stuffed agnolotti in a rich mushroom sauce; Sea scallops gently charred; Lobster poached in butter; excellent Duck. Reservations a must. Ideal choice for a special occasion. Impressive selection of regional wines. In fact, one of the best wine lists in a city with lots of them. Over 2,000 selections. Italian reds are particularly noteworthy for the depth in their list. (Over 130 Champagnes are carried.)

ARETSKY'S PATROON

160 E 46th St (bet Lexington Ave & 3rd Ave), 212-883-7373

www.patroonrestaurant.com

CUISINE: German

DRINKS: Full Bar

SERVING: Lunch, Dinner

PRICE RANGE: $$$

NEIGHBORHOOD: Midtown East

Located in a charming four-story Manhattan townhouse, this place makes every meal a celebration and even hosts rooftop cocktails. The menu consists of seasonal American favorites. Menu favorites include: 5-day Dry Aged Rib eye and Salmon with quinoa and yogurt sauce. Try the delicious creative cocktails and desserts (yummy chocolate cake and homemade ice cream).

ARMANI RISTORANTE

717 Fifth Ave, 212-207-1902

www.armani.com/restaurant/us/restaurant/armani-ristorante-5th-av/
CUISINE: Italian
DRINKS: Full bar
SERVING: Mon – Sat, lunch and dinner; only brunch on Sun
NEIGHBORHOOD: Midtown East
PRICE RANGE: $$$
This swank eatery is on the second floor of the Armani store on Fifth Avenue, hence the name. Everything is happily Italian, from the sleek waiters (clad in Armani, of course) to the fine wine list. (Don't worry, there are some bottles for less than $45).

The place is chic and slick as befitting Armani himself, who actually owns the place. That said, the price level is not $$$$, but $$$. Some of the dishes here are actually bargains when you consider the high quality on display.

You might opt for the bone-in veal chop Milanese (since that's where Armani is from). It's beyond perfection. Other hearty choices are the osso buco and the delectable cotoletta de vitello.

I got out without touching a dessert, but they looked spectacular.

AQUAVIT
65 E 55th St (bet. Madison and Park), 212-307-7311
www.aquavit.org
CUISINE: Scandinavian
DRINKS: Full bar
SERVING: Lunch, Dinner
NEIGHBORHOOD: Midtown South

PRICE RANGE: $$$$
Long a respected entry among top-rated Manhattan restaurants, here in this cool, subdued atmosphere you'll get to experience really interesting food. For lunch, try the Swedish meatballs or gravlax from the a la carte menu. There's a 4-course prix fixe menu at dinner or a 7-course tasting menu.

BENOIT
60 W 55th St (bet. Fifth & Sixth Aves), 646-943-7373
www.benoitny.com
CUISINE: French
DRINKS: Full Bar
SERVING: Lunch & Dinner
PRICE RANGE: $$$
NEIGHBORHOOD: Midtown
One of Midtown's popular spots for a "power lunch," this is a great place for lunch or dinner. Menu favorites include: Duck and Foie Gras Terrine with Pear and Apple Chutney and Traditional Cassoulet

with Bacon, Sausage, Belly, and Duck Confit.
Delicious desserts. (Try to nab a table in the bar
area—much more interesting than the dining room.)

BLUE BOTTLE COFFEE
1 Rockefeller Plaza, Concourse Level, 510-653-3394
www.bluebottlecoffee.com
CUISINE: Coffee & Tea
DRINKS: No Booze
SERVING: Lunch & Dinner
PRICE RANGE: $$
NEIGHBORHOOD: Rockefeller Center
Great coffeeshop with several New York locations.
This one is tucked away underground on the
Concourse Level located just around the corner from
the ice skating rink. Serves up a variety of coffees and
treats like granola, yogurt parfaits, and pastries. You
can walk east underground and when you come out,
you'll be in front of Saks Fifth Avenue.

BOUCHON BAKERY
Shops at Columbus Circle
10 Columbus Circle, 212-823-9366
www.bouchonbakery.com
CUISINE: Bakery, American
DRINKS: Full Bar
SERVING: Lunch & Dinner
PRICE RANGE: $$
NEIGHBORHOOD: Midtown West

A bakery and café combination located on the third floor. Menu favorites include the classic grilled cheese, the ham & cheese baguette and grilled chicken. Great desserts like dark chocolate soufflé. Oh, and if you're in need of a bathroom break, sneak in here. They have restrooms on the second and third floors.

THE BRESLIN
16 W 29th St (bet. Broadway & 5th Ave), 212-679-1939
www.breslinnyc.com
CUISINE: Steakhouse/Gastropub
DRINKS: Full Bar
SERVING: Breakfast, Lunch, & Dinner
PRICE RANGE: $$$
NEIGHBORHOOD: Midtown West/Flatiron
Located in the Ace Hotel, this high-end British gastropub offers an impressive menu. The Lamb burger is the house specialty (topped with cumin

mayo & feta) served on a ciabatta roll, but the real favorites are the Bunyanesque pig dishes. Popular hangout. Dark and crowded and lots of fun.

BURGER JOINT
Le Parker Meridian Hotel
119 W 56th St (bet. Sixth & Seventh Aves), 212-708-7414
www.burgerjointny.com
CUISINE: American, Burgers
DRINKS: Beer & Wine
SERVING: Lunch & Dinner
PRICE RANGE: $$
NEIGHBORHOOD: Midtown West
Located in Le Parker Meridian Hotel. Just follow the neon burger sign and you'll find this cute little burger joint behind velvet curtains in the lobby. Here you'll find a simple menu of burgers, fries and milkshakes but everything is tasty. And for New York, cheap.

CAFÉ AT AKA CENTRAL PARK
42 W 58th St (near Fifth Ave), 646-744-3104
www.stayaka.com
CUISINE: Gourmet Cafe
DRINKS: Full Bar
SERVING: Breakfast & Lunch
PRICE RANGE: $$
NEIGHBORHOOD: Midtown
Located in the Hotel Central Park, this café serves breakfast and lunch all day. Menu favorites include Lemon Ricotta pancakes and Smoked Salmon scrambled eggs. Everything here is made with fresh

ingredients from local farms. The décor is chic and modern giving it an upscale café ambiance.

CASA MONO
52 Irving Pl (bet. 18th St & 17th St), 212-253-2773
www.casamononyc.com
CUISINE: Spanish
DRINKS: Beer & Wine
SERVING: Lunch & Dinner
PRICE RANGE: $ to $$
NEIGHBORHOOD: Gramercy, Union Square, Flatiron
Intimate upscale eatery offering Spanish small-plate fare. The dining room has glass doors that push open in the summer months to give that al fresco feeling. Mosaic tile floors. Favorites: Soft shell crab; Hudson Valley duck; octopus with fennel & grapefruit; skirt steak with romesco; rabbit with habanero cuajada. Nice wine list, perhaps the best list of Spanish wines in the whole city. If you like sherry, this is definitely a place you'll want to visit. The sommeliers are very knowledgeable, and they've got lots of wines with excellent prices. Reservations recommended, though the best time to come is between lunch and dinner, when it's more intimate and not as crazy-hectic.

COSME
35 E 21st St (bet. Broadway & Park Ave South), 212-913-9659
www.cosmenyc.com
CUISINE: Mexican
DRINKS: Full Bar
SERVING: Lunch & Dinner

PRICE RANGE: $$$
NEIGHBORHOOD: Flatiron
Popular Mexican eatery serving locally sourced small-plates. Menu picks: Duck carnitas and Stuffed avocado. Most Mexican food made in America is just slop. Not here. Very subtle things going on. Take a bite of the tortillas served on the side and you'll realize the kind of crapy tortillas you've had before and thought were "Mexican." Great selection of artisanal spirits. Churros prepared to perfection for dessert.

CRAFT
43 E 19th St (bet. Park Ave S. & Broadway), 212-780-0880
www.craftrestaurantsinc.com/
CUISINE: American
DRINKS: Full bar
SERVING: Dinner from 5:30
NEIGHBORHOOD: Flatiron District
PRICE RANGE: $$$$
Soft-shell crabs if they have them. The best. Otherwise, loin of rabbit, braised short ribs, a 30-day dry-aged sirloin served with bone marrow, pork ravioli.

DECO FOOD + DRINK

231 W 39th St (bet. 7th Ave & 8th Ave), 646-993-1650

https://thedeconewyork.com

CUISINE: Food Court

DRINKS: Full bar

SERVING: Breakfast, Lunch, and Dinner

PRICE RANGE: $$$

NEIGHBORHOOD: Garment District / Midtown West

Art Deco inspired food hall that celebrates the many cultures of New York offering a variety of cuisines including Mexican, Afghan, French rotisserie, Hawaiian rotisserie, Brazilian, Roman Pizza, French, Sandwiches, and Pastries. Lots of varied seating choices, from communal tables to single tables to a lounge-like area with comfortable plush chairs and coffee tables.

DEL FRISCO'S DOUBLE EAGLE STEAK HOUSE
1221 Ave of the Americas, 212-575-5129
www.delfriscos.com
CUISINE: Steakhouse/American (New)/Seafood
DRINKS: Full Bar
SERVING: Lunch & Dinner
PRICE RANGE: $$$$
NEIGHBORHOOD: Theater District, Midtown West
Luxurious chain eatery specializing focusing on steaks and seafood. The big dining space is 3-stories and very dramatic with its dominating bar. Written into the dark wood is a motto: "Do Right & Fear No Man." The wine list is perhaps the very best among ALL New York steakhouses, and its exhaustive selection of California cabernets is the deepest of ANY New York restaurant. Favorites: Filet medallions or any of the prime steak cuts, Pan-seared salmon from the Bay of Fundy, Roasted chicken that's tender and juicy, Lobster Mac and Cheese. Signature cocktails. Everything is good. Reservations recommended.

DOCKS OYSTER BAR
633 Third Ave, 212-986-8080
www.docksoysterbar.com/
CUISINE: Seafood
DRINKS: Full bar
SERVING: Lunch, Dinner, Brunch
NEIGHBORHOOD: Murray Hill; Midtown South
PRICE RANGE: $$$$
All things seafood. Steamer clams, lobster, pan roasted Dover sole, Maine lobster risotto, seafood gumbo, maki and hand rolls, great raw bar. If you can't get to the Oyster Bar in Grand Central, come here instead.

ELEVEN MADISON PARK
11 Madison Ave, 212-889-0905
www.elevenmadisonpark.com/
CUISINE: American, French
DRINKS: Full bar
SERVING: Lunch, Dinner
NEIGHBORHOOD: Flatiron District

PRICE RANGE: $$$$
They jumped to a fixed-price menu to shake things up a while ago, so it's $195 for the whole meal. This is one of the most celebrated restaurants in New York, if a little fussy and self-important. (It's not fun to come here, but it's interesting.)

EMPELLON
510 Madison Ave (bet. 52nd St & 53rd St), 212-858-9365
www.empellon.com
CUISINE: Mexican
DRINKS: Full Bar
SERVING: Breakfast, Lunch, & Dinner; open 24 hours
PRICE RANGE: $$$
NEIGHBORHOOD: Midtown East
Excellent upscale Spanish eatery. Favorites: Gnocchi and Skirt steak. Impressive wine selection.

ESCA
402 W 43rd St (bet. 9th & 10th Aves.), 212-564-7272
www.esca-nyc.com/
CUISINE: Italian; other influences
DRINKS: Full bar
SERVING: Lunch, Dinner
NEIGHBORHOOD: Midtown West / Hell's Kitchen
PRICE RANGE: $$$$
Fritto misto (fried mixed seafood platter), Sicilian style fish stew, whole pan roasted black flounder, pink snapper with black lava salt.

GRAMERCY TAVERN

42 E 20th St (bet. Broadway & S Park Ave), 212-477-0777

www.gramercytavern.com

CUISINE: American (New)
DRINKS: Full Bar
SERVING: Lunch & Dinner
PRICE RANGE: $$$$
NEIGHBORHOOD: Flatiron

Well known tavern featuring a wonderful fixed-price-only menu as well as great a la carte choices. This bar is one of the most fun and busiest in New York. The more casual tavern up front gives way to a more expensive dining room in the rear, so you get to choose from 2 different experiences. People even dress differently in the 2 rooms. But either one is great. Favorites: Duck breast & sausage, Grilled shrimp & dumplings, Corn tortellini, Pea shoot salad and their famed burger. Very good vegetarian dishes available. Great dessert selection. Favorites: Busy bar scene. Creative desserts – try the cookie tray.

GRAND CENTRAL OYSTER BAR

Grand Central Station: 212-490-6650
www.oysterbarny.com
CUISINE: Seafood
DRINKS: Full bar
SERVING: Lunch, Dinner
NEIGHBORHOOD: Midtown
PRICE RANGE: $$$

This is more than a restaurant. To me, it's a quintessential New York attraction. And to me, there's nothing remotely "touristy" about it, though of course you'll find a lot of tourists here. You'll also find hundreds of business people making deals and talking loud and in the process of living in New York. This is what it looks like. Counter seating is better because you get to talk to the servers and other people sitting at the counter in a way you won't naturally do at a table. (One of the reasons I favor eating at bars rather than tables whenever I can.) I much preferred the old location upstairs, but this one is fine if you never experienced the original.

THE GRILL
99 E 52nd St (bet. Madison Ave & Park Ave), 212-375-9001
www.thegrillnewyork.com
CUISINE: American (Traditional)
DRINKS: Full Bar
SERVING: Dinner; Closed Sun
PRICE RANGE: $$$$
NEIGHBORHOOD: Midtown East
Located in the Seagram Building, this upscale steakhouse serves classic American cuisine. They have a tough act to follow, since this was where the famed Four Seasons was located. You get the feeling that they might be trying too hard, with an emphasis on over-the-top techniques. Is it really necessary for the roast beef to be sliced tableside? (It's really good, too, with the mustard rub.) The crab cakes are made with no breading at all. Very nice. Pasta la Presse and Prime Rib. Don't leave without trying the Peach Melba (again, prepared tableside). This is an unforgettable dining experience. Impressive wine list.

HAN BAT
53 W 35th St (near Sixth Ave), 212-629-5588
www.nychanbat.com
CUISINE: Korean
DRINKS: Beer & Wine
SERVING: Lunch, Dinner
PRICE RANGE: $$
NEIGHBORHOOD: Koreatown
Very popular Korean eatery. Intimate and often crowded. This 24-hour eatery serves typical Korean fare like crispy pancakes with squid and mandoo, crispy half-moon-shaped dumplings.

IPPUDO WESTSIDE
321 W 51st St (bet. 9th Ave & 8th Ave), 212-974-2500
www.ippudony.com
CUISINE: Ramen
DRINKS: Full Bar
SERVING: Lunch & Dinner
PRICE RANGE: $$

NEIGHBORHOOD: Theater District, Midtown West, Hell's Kitchen
Stylish eatery offering a menu of Japanese small plates, ramen and upscale sake. Known for their Ipudo. Other favorites: Maguro tartare and Seasonal Shoyu ramen. Usually packed and there's often a wait.

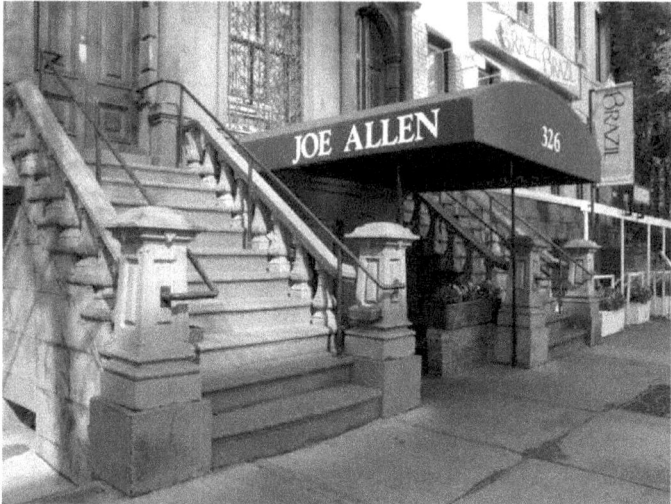

JOE ALLEN
326 W 46th St (bet. Eighth & Ninth Aves.), 212-581-6464
www.joeallenrestaurant.com
CUISINE: American comfort food
DRINKS: full bar
SERVING: lunch, dinner
NEIGHBORHOOD: Midtown West / Theatre District
PRICE RANGE: $$$
As a writer (I write novels and movies as well as travel books), I am at the theatre a lot, and it's a rare

visit to New York that I don't slip into Joe Allen for lunch or dinner or both. His burger made Joe famous long before burgers were big business. His steak tartare is among the best in town. This is the only place I know that has calf's liver on the menu every day. (Get it with bacon and onions, of course.) Meatloaf and mashed potatoes. Take a look at the Broadway posters on the wall. Ever heard of the shows? Probably not. Joe only puts up posters of shows that were flops.

JUE LAN CLUB
49 W 20th St (bet. Avenue of the Americas & 5th Ave), 646-524-7409
www.juelanclub.com
CUISINE: Chinese
DRINKS: Full Bar
SERVING: Lunch & Dinner
PRICE RANGE: $$$
NEIGHBORHOOD: Flatiron
Remember the old nightclub Limelight that was housed in a former church? Now it's a glitzy stylish eatery offering a menu of modern (Americanized) Chinese cuisine. There's a garden with lot of shade where you can eat in good weather. Favorites: Chicken kao pao and Wong tong. Great cocktails. Ice cream and sorbet for desserts.

JUNOON
27 W 24th St (bet. Fifth & Sixth Ave), 212-490-2100
www.junoonnyc.com/
CUISINE: Indian
DRINKS: Full bar

SERVING: Lunch, Dinner
NEIGHBORHOOD: Midtown South
PRICE RANGE: $$$
Two dining rooms here, one somewhat Spartan, the other more lavish. You've never had Indian food like this back home. About the best New York has to offer.

KEENS STEAKHOUSE
72 W 36th St (near Sixth Ave), 212-947-3636.
www.keens.com
CUISINE: Steakhouse
DRINKS: Full bar
SERVING: Lunch, Dinner
NEIGHBORHOOD: Midtown West
PRICE RANGE: $$$$
One of those wonderful New York experiences, open since 1885. They're famous for a huge mutton chop

that can feed 4 (but it can't feed 4 if I'm around!). On
the dining room ceiling you'll see their collection of
churchwarden pipes. The pipes were long and thin
and too delicate to be carried in a bag, so patrons left
their pipes here to be brought to them when they
finished a meal so they could smoke. Members of
Keens's Pipe Club have included everybody from
Theodore Roosevelt to Will Rogers and Babe Ruth,
architect Stanford White, Douglas MacArthur. With a
legendary reputation, this is Manhattan's best-known
USDA Prime-only steakhouse. You may know
Capital Grille in your hometown, or Morton's or any
of many other steakhouses, but in Manhattan, it's
Keens. (It's also the oldest steakhouse in the city, and
when you walk in, you'll understand what I'm saying:
it's like going back in time.) Great décor. For dessert
it's almost obligatory to get the classic New York
cheesecake. Before Keens was Keens, it was part of
the theatrical club called the **Lambs Club**, whose
manager was Albert Keen.

KINGSIDE
124 W 57th St, 212-707-8000
www.kingside-restaurant.com
CUISINE: New American
DRINKS: Full bar
SERVING: Breakfast, Lunch, Dinner
NEIGHBORHOOD: Midtown
PRICE RANGE: $$$
Located in the Viceroy Hotel, this new restaurant
from Chef Marc Murphy is slated for a fall (2013)
opening. The menu will feature items like lamb brains
dressed in capers, lemon and brown butter.

KOCHI
652 10th Ave (bet. 45th St & 46th St), 646-478-7308
www.kochinyc.com
CUISINE: Korean
DRINKS: BYOB
SERVING: Dinner; Closed Mondays
PRICE RANGE: $$
NEIGHBORHOOD: Hell's Kitchen, Midtown West
Cozy Korean eatery with an open kitchen offering
both *a al carte* and tasting menus. The 9-course
tasting meal is a must for newbies. Favorites: Raw
scallops and Chicken with aged shitake mushrooms.
Reservations recommended. **Note: BYOB.**

L'AMICO
EVENTI HOTEL
849 6th Ave (bet. W 29th & 30th Sts), 212-201-4065
www.lamico.nyc
CUISINE: Italian
DRINKS: Full Bar

SERVING: Lunch, Dinner and weekend brunch
PRICE RANGE: $$
NEIGHBORHOOD: Midtown West
This rustic-chic eatery offers a menu of pizza and creative Italian fare. There are 2 brick ovens sheathed in copper. One is used exclusively to turn out brick-oven pizzas and brunch specials like French toast and Shaksuka. The other is used to finish off chickens and steaks. Attracts a young crowd. They also provide the food for the adjacent Eventi Hotel, with an area that opens onto a big outdoor seating area with a movie screen, available weather permitting.

LA SIRENA
88 Ninth Ave (bet. 16th St & 17th St), 212-977-6096
www.lasirena-nyc.com
CUISINE: Italian/Tapas Bar
DRINKS: Full Bar
SERVING: Dinner, Lunch on Sat & Sun

PRICE RANGE: $$$
NEIGHBORHOOD: Chelsea
Located on the Plaza Level of the **Maritime Hotel**, this elegant eatery offers two distinct dining experiences – the barroom is the Tapas Bar or the main dining room for a more formal experience. Traditional Italian fare. Favorites: Blackened pulpo and Patatas bravas (classic Spanish tapa). Gluten-free options. Nice wine selection.

THE LAMBS CLUB
132 W 44th St, 212-997-5262
www.thelambsclub.com
CUISINE: American
DRINKS: Full Bar
SERVING: Breakfast, Lunch, Dinner
PRICE RANGE: $$$$
NEIGHBORHOOD: Midtown West

This place attracts all kinds of interesting folks, from editors and publishers from Conde Nast and Hearst, execs from HBO (with offices nearby) and Broadway producers looking for angels. They're all dressed very nicely either because they can afford to or because they have to. The chef here offers carefully crafted menus that make dining here a special and often a decadent experience. Menu favorites include: Chicken Cobb salad and Nova Scotia lobster roll. Live jazz every Tuesday and Wednesday, Sunday Jazz Brunch. Check website for special events. This is one of those rare great restaurants also open for breakfast (get the huevos rancheros).

LE BERNARDIN
155 W 51st St (bet. Sixth & Seventh Ave), 212-554-1515
www.le-bernardin.com
CUISINE: Seafood, French
DRINKS: Full bar
SERVING: Lunch weekdays, Dinner
NEIGHBORHOOD: Midtown West
PRICE RANGE: $$$$
I will always opt for a saddle of lamb or a simple veal chop over any fish when I'm out, but you owe it to yourself to experience the Dover sole here. It's swimming not in water where it was caught, but in butter, sauced so beautifully that it takes your breath away. Melts in your mouth. Everything else about Le Bernardin is sublimity itself. Chef Eric Ripert assumed the duties here (1991) on the untimely death of Gilbert Le Coze who came to New York and showed American chefs a new way to cook that the

smartest among them have tried to copy. Ripert stays one-step ahead of them in this beautiful temple to culinary excellence.

LE COQ RICO
30 E 20th St (bet. Broadway & Park Ave South), 212-267-7426
www.lecoqriconyc.com
CUISINE: Brasserie / French
DRINKS: Full Bar
SERVING: Lunch & Dinner
PRICE RANGE: $$$
NEIGHBORHOOD: Flatiron
Popular French bistro offering a creative menu of sophisticated poultry dishes. They had to do some research to find the right American bird that would come close to the French poulet de Bresse. Favorites: Le Coq Rico and Chicken terrine. Great upscale dining experience. Delicious desserts.

LINCOLN RISTORANTE
142 W 65th St, 212-359-6500
www.lincolnristorante.com
CUISINE: Italian
DRINKS: Full Bar
SERVING: Lunch & Dinner
PRICE RANGE: $$$
NEIGHBORHOOD: Upper West Side / Lincoln Center
Right in Lincoln Center, this sleek and modern place is stunning, but the big deal here is not the décor, it's the delicious Italian fare. Menu favorites include: Parpadelle with truffles and lamb served over creamy

polenta. Wine list is totally Italian. The chef here, Jonathan Benno, used to work at **Per Se**.

MAREA
240 Central Park S, 212-582-5100
www.marea-nyc.com
CUISINE: Italian/Seafood
DRINKS: Full Bar
SERVING: Lunch & Dinner
PRICE RANGE: $$$$
NEIGHBORHOOD: Midtown West
Upscale (but remarkably unstuffy) Italian eatery offering a menu of superior housemade pastas and seafood. From its sunken dining room, you can gaze at Central Park across the street through the big windows lining the room. There's a quieter dining room behind the busy bar. Newbies should try the Prix Fixe menu to appreciate the full range this kitchen covers. Favorites: Strozzapreti (a seafood medley with lump crab meat, sea urchin and basil over wonderful pasta), Lobster burrata and Steelhead trout. Delicious Italian desserts.

MARTA
29 E 29th St (bet. Madison Ave & Park Ave South), 212-651-3800
www.martamanhattan.com
CUISINE: Italian/Pizza
DRINKS: Full Bar
SERVING: Lunch & Dinner
PRICE RANGE: $$$
NEIGHBORHOOD: Flatiron, Midtown East
Casual eatery in the towering lobby of the **Martha Washington Hotel** known for their cracker-thin pizza and delicious Italian fare. Favorites: Ricotta pizza (Oven-Roasted Peaches, Aged Balsamic, Grilled

Sourdough) and Macellaio (Sopressata, Guanciale, Pork Sausage, Mozzarella, Grana Padano); rabbit meatballs; lamb mixed grill. Avoid the main entrees here. Stick with the thoroughly memorable pizza, with the thinnest crust you've ever had, bar none. Start with the rabbit meatballs while you wait for the pizza to cook in those gorgeous ovens behind the counter. Great cocktails. Usually crowded.

MICHAEL'S
24 W 55th St (bet. Avenue of the Americas & Fifth Ave), 212-767-0555
www.michaelsnewyork.com
CUISINE: American
DRINKS: Full Bar
SERVING: Breakfast, Lunch, Dinner
PRICE RANGE: $$$$

NEIGHBORHOOD: Midtown West
Open since 1989, this restaurant has been a popular meeting spot for media moguls and industry insiders. Big shot editors and publishers from "Old Media" lunch here, as well as billionaire real estate tycoons and the like. Nothing special about the décor here. Floral arrangements and a maroon carpet. If you weren't a first-time visitor here, you'd never notice the art on the walls. The best table in the house is #1, an 8-seat table squeezed into the window alcove. Even if you don't recognize who's sitting there, trust me, they are Somebody. Guests dine on a menu featuring haute California cuisine (things like egg white omelets with tomatoes, mushrooms and onions) and slurp down wines from an award-winning list. Menu favorites include: Smoked Salmon Pizza and Long Island Duck Breast.

MOMOSAN RAMEN & SAKE
342 Lexington Ave (39th St), 646-201-5529
www.momosanramen.com
CUISINE: Ramen
DRINKS: Full Bar
SERVING: Lunch & Dinner; Dinner only on Sunday
PRICE RANGE: $$
NEIGHBORHOOD: Murray Hill, Midtown East
Popular Ramen eatery with communal tables and an impressive selection of sakes. Favorites: Tontoksu ramen and Toppogi-rice cakes.

MONKEY BAR
60 E 54th St (at Fifth Ave), 212-288-1010
www.monkeybarnewyork.com
CUISINE: American
DRINKS: Full Bar
SERVING: Lunch & Dinner
PRICE RANGE: $$$
NEIGHBORHOOD: Midtown East / Rockefeller
Center
Nice dining establishment with an old school feel and
comfortable atmosphere. The world-famous murals
are by Edward Sorel and depict famous New Yorkers
from the 1920s and '30s. See how many you can pick
out. You'll see Fats Waller, Jack Dempsey, Irving
Berlin, Cole Porter, 3 Fitzgeralds (F. Scott, Ella and
Zelda), Condé Nast, Henry Luce, 60 personalities
altogether. Menu favorites include: Halibut and
Roasted Duck. For dessert you can create your own
ice cream specialty with a variety of toppings. This
place has a popular bar area.

THE NOMAD
NoMad Hotel
1170 Broadway (28th St), 347-472-5660.
thenomadhotel.com/#/dining
CUISINE: American
DRINKS: full bar
SERVING: lunch-dinner
NEIGHBORHOOD: Midtown South
PRICE RANGE: $$$
Never has chicken tasted so good. They serve the
whole chicken for 2. You'll love it. Why? Because
it's stuffed with foie gras and truffles. (At lunch, you
can get a chicken sandwich sliced from one of these
birds.) Also: suckling pig is compressed to intensify
the flavor; tagliatelle with crab meat, Building goes
back to 1903, so it's quite charming. This is a hard
spot to get a

table, but if you stay in the hotel, you're supposed to
get preferred seating.

PALM TOO
840 Second Ave (E 45th St), 212-687-5198
www.thepalm.com
CUISINE: Steakhouse, Seafood
DRINKS: Full bar
SERVING: Lunch, Dinner
NEIGHBORHOOD: Midtown East
PRICE RANGE: $$$$
Steaks, chops and seafood in a wonderful old New York setting. Get the porcini rubbed New York strip steak, 24 oz. Lamb and veal chops are great. Maine lobster. Crusty old waiters.

PER SE
Time Warner Center
10 Columbus Circle, 212-823-9335
www.perseny.com
CUISINE: French
DRINKS: Full bar
SERVING: Dinner nightly, Lunch (Fri – Sun)
NEIGHBORHOOD: Midtown West
PRICE RANGE: $$$$+
Famed Chef **Thomas Keller** is behind this place, considered to be one of the best restaurants in the world. The menu is fixed, so you can expect a dizzying array of delectable masterpieces. (When you finish, the waiter will bring by a box containing handmade chocolates—they'll explain to you what the filling is in each one—a nice touch to wrap up a memorable evening.)

POLO BAR

1 E 55th St (Fifth Ave), 212-207-8562
www.ralphlauren.com
CUISINE: American (Traditional)
DRINKS: Full Bar
SERVING: Dinner, Lunch
PRICE RANGE: $$$
NEIGHBORHOOD: Midtown East
One of the posh gathering places for New York's elite
is designer Ralph Lauren's lavishly decorated eatery
offering a menu of classic American fare. Bar is
upstairs, dining room is downstairs in the basement—
no windows, but brilliantly conceived. If you can
snag a table, don't be surprised when you see
celebrities. The same kind of people go here that go
to the Modern, the Monkey Bar and Michael's. Chef
Eric Ripert said the downstairs dining room was "the
best-lighted restaurant" in New York. Menu picks:
Ralph's corned beef sandwich (as famous here as the
chicken hash is at the **21 Club**) and Pigs in a blanket.
Nice selection of wines. Reservations required, unless
you get *really* lucky and walk in to find an open table.

SARDI'S
234 W 44th St (near Broadway), 212-221-8440
www.sardis.com
CUISINE: American
DRINKS: Full Bar
SERVING: Lunch, Dinner
PRICE RANGE: $$$
NEIGHBORHOOD: Midtown West / Theatre District
This iconic restaurant, located in the heart of New York's Theater District, serves lunch and dinner every day except Sunday and Monday. Great dining before and after the theatre and you might even see a Broadway star. It's a tradition for the cast to drop into Sardi's after their opening night performance to celebrate. Check out the famous cartoon celebrity sketches on the walls. (If they try to seat you upstairs, don't let them, and opt for a drink at the bar on the right just as you enter.)

SEN SAKANA
28 W 44th St (bet. Avenue of the Americas & 5th Ave), 212-221-9560
www.sensakana.com
CUISINE: Sushi/Japanese/ Peruvian
DRINKS: Full Bar
SERVING: Lunch & Dinner; Dinner only on Sat & Sun
PRICE RANGE: $$$
NEIGHBORHOOD: Midtown West
Upscale eatery offering a large menu of Japanese-Peruvian fare including Nikkei cuisine. Picks: Acevichado Makis and Tiradito Madai. Also ceviche & sushi. Impressive bar menu.

SERRA ALPINA BY LA BIRRERIA
Eataly
200 Fifth Ave (near 24th St), 212-937-8910
Across from Madison Square Park
www.eataly.com/nyc-birreria
CUISINE: Italian
DRINKS: Beer & Wine
SERVING: Lunch, Dinner
PRICE RANGE: $
NEIGHBORHOOD: Flatiron District
This is Mario Batali's Eataly's rooftop beer bar that has a great selection of beer and wines. Food choices are fresh and tasty. Menu favorites include: Piato Misto and Roasted maitake, oyster, and white beech mushrooms, encircled by young pea shoots and topped by fresh burrata. I love their excellent sausages. Casual dining at its best with great views. Though everything else in Eataly is pretty costly, you

can get away cheaper up here if you're careful. The ingredients may come from America, but the recipes are Italian. Note that there are 9 restaurants in Eataly alone, each with a distinct personality and menu of its own. You could wander in here and spend a week, never seeing anything that New York has to offer, and I'm sure that's what Mario and his backers had in mind when they opened this splendidly gargantuan place.

SUSHI GINZA ONODERA
461 Fifth Ave (bet. 41st & 40th Sts), 212-390-0925
www.sushiginzaonoderanewyork.com
CUISINE: Japanese/Sushi
DRINKS: Full Bar
SERVING: Lunch & Dinner, Dinner only on Sat; closed Sunday
PRICE RANGE: $$$$
NEIGHBORHOOD: Midtown East
Upscale eatery offering omakase-only sushi. Everything is flown in from Tokyo fish market several times a week so you know it's fresh. Menu picks: Yellow jack with lemon juice and Japanese barracuda. Tasty miso soup. Tip included in price of meal.

SUSHI SEKI
365 W 46th St (bet. 9th Ave & 8th Ave), 212-262-8880
www.sushiseki.com
CUISINE: Sushi/Japanese
DRINKS: Full Bar
SERVING: Dinner; closed Sunday

PRICE RANGE: $$$
NEIGHBORHOOD: Midtown West, Hell's Kitchen, Theater District
Beautiful upscale eatery that offers a varied menu of Japanese cuisine and sushi. Downstairs has a long marble bar for drinks and lighter fare and a communal table and tasting menus. Upstairs is for sushi, private tatami rooms, a sushi bar and tables for omakase. Favorites: Uni sushi and Ootoro sashimi. Great desserts. Reservations recommended.

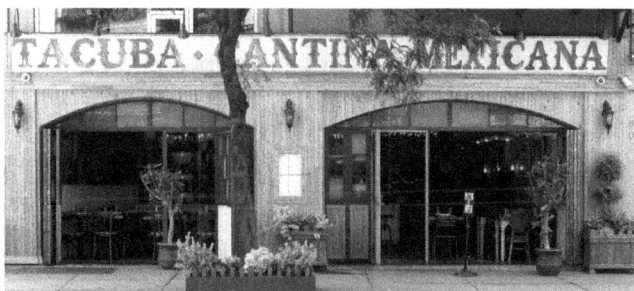

TACUBA
802 9th Ave (55th St), 212-245-4500
www.tacubanyc.com
CUISINE: Mexican/Latin American
DRINKS: Full Bar
SERVING: Lunch & Dinner
PRICE RANGE: $$
NEIGHBORHOOD: Theater District, Hell's Kitchen, Midtown West
Popular cantina offering a great assortment of classic Mexican fare. Menu picks: Quesadilla de flor (burrata, zucchini flower, and a kale pesto) and Fried Brussels sprouts and short rib quesadilla. Large selection of Tequilas and Mezcal. (They also deliver)

TEMERARIO

198 8th Ave (bet. 21st St & 20th St), 212-645-2100
www.temerarionyc.com
CUISINE: Mexican
DRINKS: Full Bar
SERVING: Lunch & Dinner; Weekend Brunch
PRICE RANGE: $$
NEIGHBORHOOD: Chelsea
Popular eatery offering a creative menu of typical
Mexican street food interpreted broadly. Menu picks:
Mahi Mahi fish tacos and Chorizo queso fundido
topped with avocado. Happy hour specials. Tasty
margaritas.

UPLAND

345 Park Ave S (bet. 26th St & 25th St), 212-686-
1006
www.uplandnyc.com
CUISINE: American (New)

DRINKS: Full Bar
SERVING: Lunch & Dinner
PRICE RANGE: $$$
NEIGHBORHOOD: Flatiron
Spacious, trendy brasserie featuring a menu of American cuisine with California and Italian influences. Nice selection of pizzas, steaks, and fish dishes. The Duck special stole the show. Great cocktails and tasty desserts. (Upland is the California town where the chef is from.)

VIA BRASIL
34 W 46 St (bet. Fifth & Sixth Aves), 212-997-1158
www.viabrasilrestaurant.com
CUISINE: Brazilian
DRINKS: Full Bar
SERVING: Lunch, Dinner
PRICE RANGE: $$
NEIGHBORHOOD: Midtown
You've heard of New York's Little Italy (Nolita), Chinatown and Koreatown, right? Well, there's a Little Brazil as well. When I say little, I mean it: it's scarcely a block long and it's here in Midtown. It makes for a nice (if offbeat) place for a celebration or a business meal. Menu favorites include: Shredded baked codfish and Grilled Salmon and pineapple sauce. Brazilian specialties are tasty too, like the "feijoada completa," which is a hefty stew made of black beans and chunks of pork that's become the national dish of the country.

WISEFISH POKÉ
263 W 19th St (bet. 7th Ave & 8th Ave), 212-367-7653
www.wisefishpoke.com
CUISINE: Seafood/Hawaiian
DRINKS: No Booze
SERVING: Lunch & Dinner
PRICE RANGE: $$
NEIGHBORHOOD: Chelsea
Counter service eatery offering creative menu of Hawaiian cuisine. You can put together your own poké dish from the menu. Lots of fish dishes. Favorites: Ahi tuna and Spicy tuna (both tasty and very different).

Midtown Budget Spots

2ND AVE DELI
162 E 33rd St (bet. Lexington Ave & 3rd Ave), 212-689-9000
www.2ndavedeli.com
CUISINE: Deli/Kosher
DRINKS: Beer & Wine
SERVING: Breakfast, Lunch, Dinner
PRICE RANGE: $$
NEIGHBORHOOD: Murray Hill, Kips Bay, Midtown East

Popular deli for decades known for their great overstuffed sandwiches. Yiddish theatre posters adorn the walls. Tiled floor, T-shirts, cookbooks. This is the place to get tongue and chopped liver. Of course they serve Matzoh Ball soup. Jellied calves feet.

ACUARIO CAFÉ
306 W 37th St (bet. 9th Ave & 8th Ave), 212-564-9040
www.acuariocafe.wordpress.com
CUISINE: Latin American
DRINKS: No Booze
SERVING: Breakfast & Lunch; closed Sun
PRICE RANGE: $
NEIGHBORHOOD: Midtown West, Hell's Kitchen
Located inside of a loading dock, this hole-in-the-wall café offers a menu of Latin American cuisine and attracts quite a diverse crowd (mostly blue collar working class). Favorites: Central American chicken; fried fish; beef stew; and fresh fish with rice and beans. Eat in or take-away. Cash only. Nothing over $10.

BAOHAUS
238 E 14th St, 646-669-8889,
www.baohausnyc.com
CUISINE: Taiwanese
DRINKS: No Booze
SERVING: Lunch, Dinner, Late Night
NEIGHBORHOOD: Gramercy, East Village
PRICE RANGE: $
This small Taiwanese sandwich shop sells gourmet
eats at cheap prices. Every bao is made from
hormone-free meat or organic tofu. Try dishes like
the Chairman Bao, stuffed with pork belly.

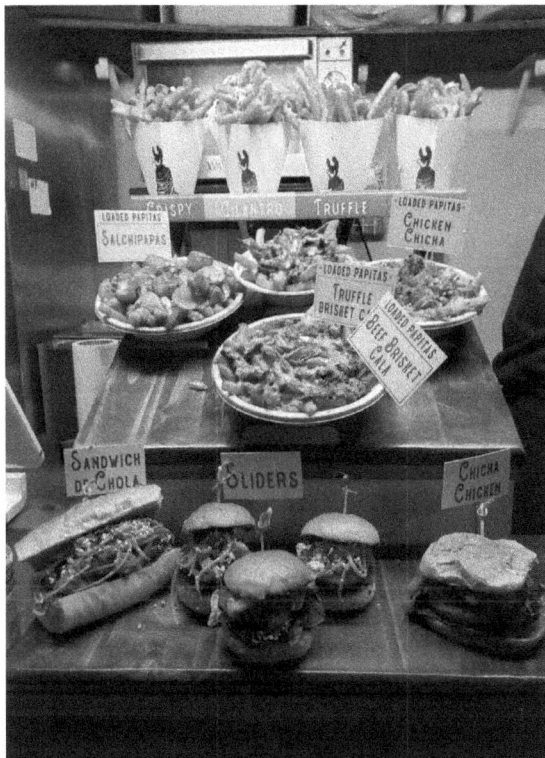

BOLIVIAN LLAMA PARTY
Turnstyle Underground Market
1000 S Eighth Ave (cor. 57th St), 347-395-5481
http://www.blp.nyc/
CUISINE: Latin American/Food Stand
DRINKS: No Booze
SERVING: Lunch & Dinner
PRICE RANGE: $
NEIGHBORHOOD: Hell's Kitchen, Midtown West
Located underneath Columbus Circle in the subway
tunnel where there are some shops, this compact
restaurant serves Bolivian specialties, traditional and

modern. Specialties are Saltenas (similar to an empanada). Favorites: Beni Beef Salteña and Chimba Chicken Salteña. Really cheap and really good.

CHEF YU
520 8th Ave (W 37th St), 212-736-6150
www.chefyu-nyc.com/
CUISINE: Chinese
DRINKS: Full bar
SERVING: Lunch, Dinner
NEIGHBORHOOD: Midtown West / Garment District
PRICE RANGE: $$
They have 15 lunch options for less than $6. And it's all tasty. Dinner is almost as cheap: pan-fried vegetable dumplings, shrimp dumplings, minced chicken and pine nuts, 5-spice roast beef, tangerine chicken, a dozen steak plates, pork, wide variety of fish and shellfish dishes, all in the $11 to $13 range. Can't go wrong here.

GREAT NORTHERN FOOD HALL
Grand Central Terminal
89 E 42nd St (bet. Park Ave & Vanderbilt Ave)
Enter at 42nd St or from the Main Concourse
https://www.greatnorthernfood.com/
CUISINE: Scandinavian/Food Court
DRINKS: Full Bar
SERVING: Breakfast, Lunch, & Dinner
PRICE RANGE: $$
NEIGHBORHOOD: Midtown East
Food hall offering six pavilions with more than 100
items, with a Nordic theme. The is a great place if
you're passing through majestic Grand Central, one
of the great landmarks in Manhattan. Soaring
architecture. Solid food and cheap. Favorites: Danish
open-faced sandwiches and Nordic risotto-style
porridges.

HAANDI
113 Lexington Ave (bet. 27th St & 28th St), 212-685-5200
http://haandiny.com/
CUISINE: Indian/Pakistani
DRINKS: No Booze
SERVING: 10 a.m. – 4 a.m.
PRICE RANGE: $
NEIGHBORHOOD: Kips Bay
Popular cheap spot serving ready-made dishes from Southeast Asia. Favorites: Chicken kabab and Dal Gosht (mutton with lentils). No frills eatery.

HIDE-CHAN RAMEN

314 W 53rd St (bet. 9th Ave & 8th Ave), 212-969-0066

248 E 57th St (bet. 2nd & 3rd Aves), 212-813-1800

http://www.hidechanramen.nyc/

CUISINE: Ramen

DRINKS: Beer & Wine

SERVING: Breakfast & Lunch; closed Sat & Sun

PRICE RANGE: $$

NEIGHBORHOOD: Theater District, Midtown West, Hell's Kitchen; also Midtown East

Small ramen shop, one on the East Side and one on the West Side, serving up favorites like black garlic noodles, pork buns & pork bone broth. Favorites: Chicken teriyaki avocado bowl and Bonito Dashi Ramen. Lunch specials. Sake cocktails and variety of beers. If you've never experienced a *real* Ramen eatery, do yourself a favor and try this one.

HILL COUNTRY CHICKEN
1123 Broadway (W 25th St), 212-257-6446
www.hillcountrychicken.com/
CUISINE: Southern
DRINKS: Beer & Wine
SERVING: Breakfast, Lunch, Dinner
NEIGHBORHOOD: Midtown South
PRICE RANGE: $$
You're coming here for fried chicken, period. Helpful staff, busy and exciting atmosphere in a fun-filled place. Bright and cheerful, with yellow being a prominent color. Cheesy mashed potatoes and don't overlook the pies.

LOS TACOS NO. 1
75 Ninth Avenue, 212-256-0343
www.lostacos1.com
CUISINE: Mexican
DRINKS: No Booze
SERVING: Lunch, Dinner
NEIGHBORGHOOD: Chelsea, Meatpacking District
PRICE RANGE: $
Located in the Chelsea Market, here you'll find authentic tacos, Adobaba tacos, deep-fried quesadillas and horchata. All made with hand-pressed tortillas. Mexican beverages.

SONS OF THUNDER
204 E 38th St (bet. 3rd Ave & Tunnel Exit St), 646-863-2212
https://www.sonsofthunder.com/
CUISINE: Hot Dogs/Poke

DRINKS: Full Bar
SERVING: Lunch & Dinner; Closed Sunday
PRICE RANGE: $$
NEIGHBORHOOD: Murray Hill, Midtown East
Casual eatery specializing in Hawaiian and
Californian flavors. Favorites: Huli Huli Teriyaki
Chicken and Salmon poke bowl. Happy Hour. The
'Times' called this "the best poke in New York." And
it's cheap!

TIFFIN WALLAH
127 E 28th St, 212-685-7301
www.tiffindelivery.us
CUISINE: South Indian, Vegetarian
DRINKS: Beer & Wine
SERVING: Lunch, Dinner
NEIGHBORHOOD: Midtown East – Kips Bay
PRICE RANGE: $$

Spicy tomato lentil soup; Punjab curries; Gujarati curries; Undhiyu; Sukhi Bhaji; Dosa (large crispy crepes served with coconut chutney and sambar); Uttapam, and lots more.

Chapter 3
UPPER EAST SIDE

DID YOU FIND AN INTERESTING PLACE?
If you discover a place you think I should check out on my next visit, drop me a line, will you? I'll mention your name if I end up listing it.
andrewdelaplaine@mac.com

ARLINGTON CLUB
1032 Lexington Ave (bet. 73rd St & 74th St), 212-249-5700
www.arlingtonclubny.com
CUISINE: Steakhouse/Sushi/American (New)
DRINKS: Full Bar
SERVING: Dinner
PRICE RANGE: $$$$
NEIGHBORHOOD: Upper East Side
Two-level eatery offering a unique menu of steakhouse fare along with sushi, salads and sides. This place, given it neighborhood, attracts a crowd with money to burn, all different ages, and has become a locals' hangout. The bar up front is where you'll wait for your table. Upstairs, the dining room,

with its soaring glass ceiling overhead, reminds you of a French railroad station. Signature items: 28-day, dry-aged Cote de Boeuf for two and Dover Sole "Modern Meuniere." Great Happy Hour deals (cheap oysters and shrimp cocktail). Upscale dining experience. Reservations recommended.

THE BAR ROOM
117 E 60th St (bet. Park Ave & Lexington Ave), 212-561-5523
www.thebarroomnyc.com
CUISINE: American (New)
DRINKS: Full bar
SERVING: Lunch & Dinner
PRICE RANGE: $$
NEIGHBORHOOD: Upper East Side
Stylish bistro offering a creative men of New American fare. Black-and-white checked tiles on the floor, a long highly polished wooden bar, red banquettes and café chairs all project a perfect bistro atmosphere. Picks: Lobster rolls and Salmon. Craft beer & classic cocktails. Can be busy but only takes reservations for large groups.

BOHEMIAN SPIRIT
321 East 73rd St (bet. 1st Ave & 2nd Ave), 212-861-1038
www.bohemianspiritrestaurant.com
CUISINE: Czech
DRINKS: Full Bar
SERVING: Dinner
PRICE RANGE: $$
NEIGHBORHOOD: Upper East Side, Yorkville

Popular Central European eatery with images of Czech celebrities adorning the walls. Serves a menu of Czech favorites like Schnitzel and Beef Goulash; beer roasted sausages; svickova (roasted beef in a cream sauce) with dumplings and cranberry; duck leg with red cabbage. Nice selection of Pilsner beer.

CAFÉ SABARSKY
Neue Galerie
1048 Fifth Ave (near 86th St), 212-288-0665
www.kurtgutenbrunner.com/restaurants/cafe-sabarsky/
CUISINE: German-Austrian
DRINKS: Beer & Wine Only
SERVING: Lunch & Dinner
PRICE RANGE: $$
NEIGHBORHOOD: Upper East Side
This Viennese-style café serves delicious German cuisine when usually what you get is very indifferent. I get through this hearty and heavy food by skipping the potatoes that seem to come with everything. Menu favorites include: Bavarian Sausage and Apple Strudel. Coffee drinks and desserts are out of this world (like the dark chocolate cake). Note that this place is inside the Neue Galerie, a wonderful showcase for German and Austrian art from the 20th Century, worth a special trip even if you don't eat here.

THE DAISY
1641 Second Ave (at E 85th St), 646-964-5756
www.thedaisynyc.com
CUISINE: American (New) / Gastropub / Mexican

DRINKS: Full Bar
SERVING: Dinner, Lunch on Sat & Sun
PRICE RANGE: $$
NEIGHBORHOOD: Yorkville, Upper East Side
Hip eatery offering a varied menu of American and Mexican fare. Favorites: Salmon & Mushrooms and Bolognese. Craft cocktails and an impressive Agave Spirits collection. Live music. Friday night live DJ.

DANIEL
60 E 65th St, 212-288-0033
www.danielnyc.com
CUISINE: French/American
DRINKS: Full Bar
SERVING: Dinner only; Closed on Sun
PRICE RANGE: $$$$
NEIGHBORHOOD: Upper East Side
Upscale Chef Boulud eatery with an impressive menu of French and American cuisine. Boulud came from the Lyon region of France, and it's hard to find anyone who serves up French cuisine better than his. His kitchen staff is rigorously trained, as are the servers in the front of the house. Only the best here. (Of course, you'll pay handsomely for it.) Go with one of the tasting menus and you can't go wrong. Boulud started out at Le Cirque in 1986, and gradually added American ideas to his menus before moving on to open his own place in the 1990s. Nice bar and lounge area. Quite formal, but not stuffy. Note: main room requires men to wear suit jackets. Reservations begin 2 months in advance. Presentation and food live up to the two-star Michelin rating.

THE EAST POLE
133 E 65th St (nr. Lexington Ave), 212-249-2222
www.theeastpolenyc.com
CUISINE: American
DRINKS: Full Bar
SERVING: Dinner only, but lunch coming soon
PRICE RANGE: $$$$
NEIGHBORHOOD: Upper East Side
A lovely new place from the people at Fat Radish
down in Chinatown. Here, however, they are
ensconced in 2 brownstones and offer seating out in a
garden under a leafy canopy. The décor is mostly
black and white, very chic but no white tablecloths.
Oysters make a good starter, but try some of their
house-made pickles, or the Scotch egg and mustard or
the roasted cauliflower with curried lentils. Grilled
striped bass or chicken Kiev make good main

courses, or try my favorite, the Fennel & Fish Pie, with lobster and tarragon.

ELI'S TABLE
1413 3rd Ave (bet. 80th St & 81st St), 212-717-9798
https://www.elizabar.com/Elis-Table.aspx
CUISINE: American (New)
DRINKS: Full Bar
SERVING: Breakfast, Lunch, & Dinner
PRICE RANGE: $$
NEIGHBORHOOD: Upper East Side/Yorkville
Upscale eatery offers a menu of New American cuisine and the best thing about this place is the endless variety and the daily changes not only in the farm-to-table menu, but in the 20 or so wines by the glass they serve. They are really on top of their wine game here. Wine pours are 2.5 or 5 ounces, or buy a whole bottle. If you live in th4 city, check out their wine courses every 2 weeks. A lot of people in the wine business frequent this place. Favorites: Tuna tartare, crispy Octopus, English pea crostini, celery & parsley salad, soft shell crabs. But, as I say, everything changes daily. Creative desserts. Weekend brunch. **Eli's Market** is next door.

FELICE
1593 First Av. (at 83rd St.), 212-249-4080
1166 First Ave (at 64th St), 212-593-2223
www.felice64.com
www.felice83.com
CUISINE: Wine bar, Italian
DRINKS: Full bar
SERVING: Lunch, Dinner, Brunch
NEIGHBORHOOD: Upper East Side
PRINCE RANGE: $$$
If you can't get to Tuscany, close your eyes and
inhale. This place will make you think you're over
there. Fish beautifully prepared, organic chicken with
bursting flavor and sliced steak. Pasta dishes are
uniformly good, as is the butternut squash risotto.
Every night the chef makes up a l'aperitivo which
includes 3 tastings to launch your experience here. If
you don't want the l'aperitivo, by all means opt for
one of the crostini.

FLORA BAR
945 Madison Ave (E 75th St), 646-558-5383
www.florabarnyc.com
CUISINE: Seafood
DRINKS: Beer & Wine
SERVING: Breakfast, Lunch, Dinner
PRICE RANGE: $$
NEIGHBORHOOD: Upper East Side
Located in the **Met Breuer** in the sunken space under
the lobby, this eclectic modern eatery offers a creative
menu focusing on seafood. Favorites: Blue shrimp
with cocktail sauce; Rutabaga & raclette tart; Steak
with beets & béarnaise; Lobster crudo and Snow crab.
Nice wine selection.

FRED'S AT BARNEY'S NEW YORK
660 Madison Ave (bet. 60th and 61st Sts), 212-833-
2200
www.barneys.com
CUISINE: American/Italian
DRINKS: Full Bar
SERVING: Lunch & Dinner

PRICE RANGE: $$$
NEIGHBORHOOD: Upper East Side
Located on the ninth floor of Barney's, this is a popular place for the "ladies who lunch" crowd. Especially the younger ladies. It also attracts a big following in the fashion and media worlds. Menu favorites include: Chicken livers and Pot roast. The Lobster Club is the best, but the chopped salad is de rigueur. It's a little loud (that's why it's so fun) and reservations are recommended.

J. G. MELON
1291 Third Ave (bet. 75th St & 74th St), 212-744-0585
https://jgmelon-nyc.com
CUISINE: American (Traditional)
DRINKS: Full Bar
SERVING: Lunch & Dinner
PRICE RANGE: $$
NEIGHBORHOOD: Upper East Side, Yorkville
Comfortable neighborhood eatery known for their succulent burgers cooked on the griddle. Been here for decades. Cash only. Bobby Flay says, "I just walk in here and a burger magically appears." Good example to follow.

JEAN-GEORGES
Trump Hotel
1 Central Park West, 212-299-3900
www.jean-georges.com
CUISINE: French / American / Asian
DRINKS: Full bar
SERVING: Lunch, Dinner
NEIGHBORHOOD: Upper West Side
PRICE RANGE: $$$$; jackets required at dinner.
Flagship of **Jean-Georges Vongerichten**. I'd go with the tasting menu either for lunch or dinner. They are good values. (They have a 3-course tasting menu or two 6-course menus.)

LA GOULUE
29 E 61st St, 212-988-8169
www.lagoulue restaurant.com
CUISINE: French
DRINKS: Full Bar
SERVING: Lunch & Dinner
PRICE RANGE: $$$
NEIGHBORHOOD: Upper East Side

Upscale French bistro is a treasured New York institution, in New York since the 1970s. This place even has the dark wood paneling from the original location, which was 4 blocks from here. They kept it in storage and installed it here when they had to move because the landlord forced them out. Most of the servers are French, which helps to throw off the ambiance of a "real" French bistro, though most French bistros don't have the snob factor as much as you get here. If they seat you in the rear, don't let it worry you. It just means you're a Nobody. But even so, it's quite an experience watching all the other 1-percenters show off, ruffle their feathers and preen. Favorites: I love the marinated herring here, as well as the haricots verts and the onion soup to start; Sole meunière is always a good choice; Steak tartare is always really good here, and the whole grilled Dorade. Impressive wine list. Make reservations. Much prefer this over **Le Bibloquet**, which is nearby, because there are fewer loud people making a fuss over themselves.

LE BILBOQUET
20 E 60th St (bet. Madison & Park), 212-751-3036
http://www.lebilboquetny.com/
CUISINE: French/Cajun/Creole
DRINKS: Full Bar
SERVING: Lunch & Dinner
PRICE RANGE: $$$
NEIGHBORHOOD: Upper East Side
Busy, bustling, cramped & trendy upscale eatery favored by the very wealthy, bold-faced names one sees in swanky Upper East Side bastians. Movie stars,

bigwigs in finance and media, you name it, they come here or **La Goulue** a hop and a skip away. Favorites: Cajun chicken is a must-have here; Filet, Fries and Creamed Spinach comes as one dish. The desserts are spectacular. It's hard to limit yourself to just one. Impressive wine list, but not for the faint of heart. Prices are ridiculous. Reservations recommended (not that they always honor them if it doesn't suit them). Snob factor is high.

PASTRAMI QUEEN
1125 Lexington Ave (bet. E 78th & 79th St), 212-734-1500
www.pastramiqueen.com
CUISINE: Deli/Kosher
DRINKS: No Booze
SERVING: Lunch & Dinner
PRICE RANGE: $$
NEIGHBORHOOD: Upper East Side
Kosher deli known for their overstuffed sandwiches. Pastrami (made on site), smoked turkey, corned beef – all worth tasting. Also deli classics like matzo balls and knishes. Limited seating.

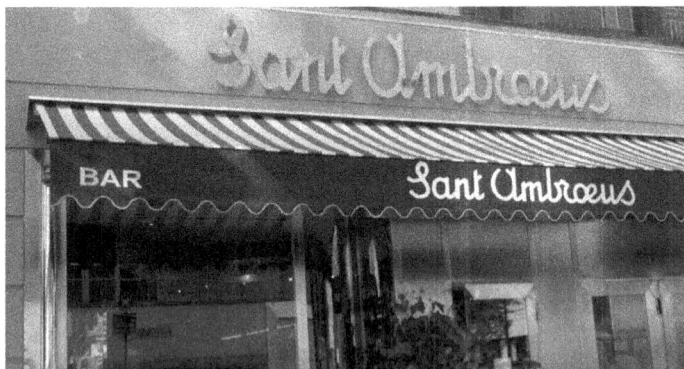

SANT AMBROEUS
1000 Madison Ave (bet. 77th & 78th Sts), 212-570-2211
www.santambroeus.com
CUISINE: Italian
DRINKS: Full Bar
SERVING: Brunch, Lunch, Dinner
PRICE RANGE: $$$
NEIGHBORHOOD: Upper East Side
A great little Italian eatery that is popular for breakfast and brunch with people in the Manhattan fashion industry. If you know who they are, you'll see a lot of famous names stroll in here for lunch. Menu favorites include: Tagliatelle in a light veal ragu and Agliatelle alla Bolognese. Great place for afternoon coffee / cappuccino and dessert. Family friendly.

SERENDIPITY 3
225 E 60th St (bet. Second & Third Aves), 212-838-3531
www.serendipity3.com
CUISINE: American, Desserts
DRINKS: No Booze
SERVING: Lunch & Dinner
PRICE RANGE: $$
NEIGHBORHOOD: Upper East Side
This iconic Upper East Side favorite of Andy Warhol still attracts crowds and there's usually a wait for tables. A favorite of kids and those who love sweets. Menu favorites are the Frozen Hot Chocolate and the giant burgers. Beyoncé and Gwyneth stop in here.

THE SIMONE
151 E 82nd St (bet. Lexington Ave & 3rd Ave), 212-772-8861
https://thesimonenyc.com
CUISINE: French
DRINKS: Full Bar
SERVING: Dinner; closed Sunday
PRICE RANGE: $$$$
NEIGHBORHOOD: Upper East Side
Upscale eatery serving classic French fare laid out on a handwritten menu. Though the atmosphere in the townhouse and the attitude of the waiters is quite formal, there's nothing stuffy about the place, nothing at all. Favorites: Duck Breast and Wild King Salmon. Delicious dessert selection. Crafted cocktails. Impressive wine list.

SISTINA
24 E 81st St (bet. 5th Ave & Madison Ave) 212-861-7660
www.sistinany.com
CUISINE: Italian
DRINKS: Full Bar
SERVING: Lunch, & Dinner; Closed Sun
PRICE RANGE: $$$$
NEIGHBORHOOD: Upper East Side
Sophisticated bistro offering a menu of classic Italian fare. Located just a block from the Metropolitan Museum of Art, it's appropriate that the walls here display Matisse and other notable artists. Don't bother looking at the menu as they always have great specials (usually around 10), and it can take the waiter more than a few minutes just to go through

them. I always order one of the specials here, never from the menu unless there's something I particularly have a yearning for, like the langoustines you can get each spring—they're grilled and seasoned beautifully. Pappardelle Sistina with veal Bolognese and wild mushrooms; Crispy-skinned branzino; Grilled octopus. Great pastas. Massive wine list.

VAUCLUSE
100 E 63rd St (Lexington Ave), 646-869-2300
www.vauclusenyc.com
CUISINE: French
DRINKS: Full Bar
SERVING: Lunch & Dinner
PRICE RANGE: $$$$
NEIGHBORHOOD: Upper East Side
Upscale brasserie serving French classics. Menu picks: Chilled roasted leeks; épaulettes, so named because they look like military shoulder decorations,

have 2 pockets of pasta—on one side is succulent rabbit, on the other, reblochon cheese—when you eat them together, you feel and taste why French food can be so sublime; Duck confit ravioli with aged Parmesan; Steaks are cooked to perfection. Desserts are rich but worth the calories. Elegant dining experience.

THE WRITING ROOM
1703 Second Ave (88th St), 212-335-0075
www.thewritingroomnyc.com
CUISINE: American
DRINKS: Full bar
SERVING: Dinner
NEIGHBORHOOD: Upper East Side; Yorkville
PRICE RANGE: $$$

This is the location of the famed restaurant Elaine's, home to hundreds of writers over the decades. It closed not too long after its eponymous owner died. Now the people from Parlor Steakhouse, Michael and Susy Glick, have reopened it. It's got the same clubby feel that Elaine's had. Smoked white fish; roasted chicken soup; veal meatloaf; fried chicken (very good); smoked prime brisket.

Upper East Side
Budget Spots

BOHEMIAN SPIRIT
321 East 73rd St (bet. 1st Ave & 2nd Ave), 212-861-1038
www.bohemianspiritrestaurant.com
CUISINE: Czech
DRINKS: Full Bar
SERVING: Dinner
PRICE RANGE: $$
NEIGHBORHOOD: Upper East Side, Yorkville
Popular Central European eatery with images of Czech celebrities adorning the walls. Serves a menu of Czech favorites like Schnitzel and Beef Goulash; beer roasted sausages; svickova (roasted beef in a cream sauce) with dumplings and cranberry; duck leg with red cabbage. Nice selection of Pilsner beer.

PASTRAMI QUEEN
1125 Lexington Ave (bet. E 78th & 79th St), 212-734-1500
www.pastramiqueen.com
CUISINE: Deli/Kosher
DRINKS: No Booze
SERVING: Lunch & Dinner
PRICE RANGE: $$
NEIGHBORHOOD: Upper East Side
Kosher deli known for their overstuffed sandwiches. Pastrami (made on site), smoked turkey, corned beef – all worth tasting. Also deli classics like matzo balls and knishes. Limited seating.

PENELOPE
159 Lexington Ave (E 30th St), 212-481-3800
www.penelopenyc.com/
CUISINE: American
DRINKS: Beer & Wine
SERVING: Breakfast, Lunch, Dinner

NEIGHBORHOOD: Midtown South; Kips Bay
PRICE RANGE: $$
Charming unpretentious place in Murray Hill where I used to live. A real family atmosphere. (Penelope is their turtle.) Chicken meatballs with pesto; curried chicken salad; Ellie's spinach pie; chicken pot pie; variety of excellent sandwiches, including my favorite the BBLT (extra bacon).

SCHALLER & WEBER
1654 2nd Ave (bet. 85th St & 86th St), 212-879-3047
www.schallerweber.com
CUISINE: Meat shop
DRINKS: No Booze
SERVING: 10 a.m. – 7 p.m.; closed Sunday
PRICE RANGE: $$
NEIGHBORHOOD: Yorkville, Upper East Side
Old-school German market & butcher shop. Here you'll find a wide variety of wieners, fresh meat, cold

cuts, cheeses, jams, bread, candy, coffee and other
sundries.

TACO MIX
234 E 116th St. (bet. 2nd & 3rd Aves.), East Harlem,
212-289-2963
www.eatrealtacos.com
CUISINE: Mexican
DRINKS: No booze
SERVING: Lunch, Dinner
NEIGHBORHOOD: Upper East Side
PRICE RANGE: $
Tacos al pastor is what you want here and they're so
good they're worth a special trip.

Chapter 4
UPPER WEST SIDE

DID YOU FIND AN INTERESTING PLACE?
If you discover a place you think I should check out
on my next visit, drop me a line, will you? I'll
mention your name if I end up listing it.
andrewdelaplaine@mac.com

AFRICA KINE
2267 7th Ave (bet. W 133rd St & w 134th St), 212-
666-9400
www.africakine.com

CUISINE: Fast Food
DRINKS: No Booze
SERVING: Lunch & Dinner
PRICE RANGE: $$
NEIGHBORHOOD: Harlem
Small eatery serving a varied menu of traditional
African comfort fare. Favorites: Lamb mate; thiebou
guinaar; Dibi chicken and Lamb with plantains. There
are too many places serving this kind of food in
America. Enjoy this on your visit. Women cook
during lunch, while at dinner the men come in for
their shift.

AMY RUTH'S
113 W 116th St (nr. Malcolm X Blvd), 212-280-8779
www.amyruths.com
CUISINE: Southern, Soul Food
DRINKS: Full Bar
SERVING: Breakfast, Lunch, Dinner daily; till 5 a.m.
on weekends
PRICE RANGE: $$
Behind an unpretentious storefront you'll find this
legendary Harlem eatery where they have a special
called "The Rev. Al Sharpton," consisting of chicken
and waffles. Braised oxtail stew; jerked chicken
Jamaica style; country chicken and dumplings;
smothered steak; honey-dipped friend chicken; BBQ
ribs; fried or baked catfish.

BARAWINE
200 Lenox Avenue (120th Street), 646-756-4154
www.barawine.com
CUISINE: French
DRINKS: Beer & Wine Only
SERVING: Lunch, Dinner
PRICE RANGE: $$$
A beautiful French restaurant with a modern look. For starters the wine selection is great with over 200 wines and the owners are often around to offer suggestions. Menu favorites include: Tuna with seaweed salad and Duck breast. Friendly service.

BARLEY & GRAIN
421 Amsterdam Avenue (between 80th St & 81st St), 646-360-3231
www.barleyandgrain.com **WEBSITE DOWN AT PRESSTIME**
NEIGHBORHOOD: Upper West Side

This place where you can get huge Porterhouse for 2 is right across the street from Tangled Vine, a wine bar owned by a couple of the partners here.

BARNEY GREENGRASS
541 Amsterdam Ave (86th St), 212-724-4707
www.barneygreengrass.com
CUISINE: Deli
DRINKS: No Booze
SERVING: 8:30 a.m. – 6 p.m.
PRICE RANGE: $$
NEIGHBORHOOD: Upper West Side
In business since 1908, this iconic Jewish deli is known for their smoked fish, and a lot of other things besides. I love their scrambled eggs and omelettes. Great breakfast and sandwiches. Try the homemade Cheese Blintzes. Get the Rugelach for dessert. Cash only.

BIN 71
237 Columbus Ave. (bet. 70th & 71st St.): 212-362-5446
www.bin71.com
CUISINE: Italian/American
DRINKS: Beer & Wine Only
SERVING: Dinner
PRICE RANGE: $$
NEIGHBORHOOD: Upper West Side
This cozy wine bar and restaurant offers a comfortable atmosphere for dining or just enjoying wine or cocktails. Menu favorites include: Roasted Chicken and Meatballs. Outdoor seating available.

BLVD BISTRO
239 Lenox Ave (122nd St), 212-678-6200
www.boulevardbistrony.com
CUISINE: American (Traditional)/Soul Food
DRINKS: Beer & Wine
SERVING: Lunch & Dinner; closed Monday
PRICE RANGE: $$
NEIGHBORHOOD: Harlem
French-American bistro set in a rustic-chic townhouse. The friend chicken is pan-fried to order, so it takes a few minutes, but is well worth it. Menu picks: Fried chicken biscuit; grouper with a crispy cornmeal crust; Crab benny; Okra is breaded lightly with cornmeal & very tasty. Great pick for weekend brunch. Nice selection of desserts and wine.

BOULUD SUD
20 W 64th St, 212-595-1313
www.bouludsud.com
CUISINE: Mediterranean

DRINKS: Full Bar
SERVING: Lunch & Dinner
PRICE RANGE: $$$
NEIGHBORHOOD: Upper West Side
Boulud has an inspired take on this menu of African inspired specialties. Menu favorites include: Lamb burger with Feta, Harissa, Eggplant, Tzatziki and Sweet Potato Chips. Delicious creative desserts like the Warm Lemon Custard served in a Tagine.

CALLE OCHO
Excelsior Hotel, 45 W 81st St, 212-873-5025
www.calleochonyc.com
CUISINE: Cuban, Latin American
DRINKS: Full Bar
SERVING: Dinner & brunch on weekends
PRICE RANGE: $$
NEIGHBORHOOD: Upper West Side
Beautiful restaurant that offers a wonderful Latin experience. Here the mojitos are the best and the sangrias are amazing. The friendly servers' recommendations are usually right on. Menu favorites include: Calamari and Paella, which was abundant and fresh. For dessert try the homemade ice cream.

CHARLES' COUNTRY PAN-FRIED CHICKEN
2461 Frederick Douglass Blvd, 212-281-1800
No Website
CUISINE: Barbeque, Southern
DRINKS: No Booze
SERVING: Lunch & Dinner
PRICE RANGE: $$
NEIGHBORHOOD: Harlem
May be the best chicken north of the Mason-Dixon.

CORNER SOCIAL
321 Lenox Ave, 212-510-8552
www.cornersocialnyc.com
CUISINE: American
DRINKS: Full Bar
SERVING: Lunch & Dinner, Brunch

PRICE RANGE: $$
NEIGHBORHOOD: Harlem
Great spot for brunch with delicious offerings like
Plaintain bread (a tasty take on banana bread) and
Chicken and Pancakes. How about this for an artery-
clogging selection: deep fried mac & cheese
croquettes served with truffle mayo? Cheeseburger
spring rolls? Bring 'em on. Most dishes come with
free coffee. No reservations for brunch so come early.

DEAD POET
450 Amsterdam Ave. (bet. 81st & 82nd Sts.): 212-
595-5670
www.thedeadpoet.com
CUISINE: Bar Snacks
DRINKS: Full Bar
SERVING: Lunch & Dinner
PRICE RANGE: $$
NEIGHBORHOOD: Upper West Side
Popular café frequented by the artsy crowd but for
people watching. Good selection of beers, bottle and
tap. Friendly service. Menu includes typical bar food
like burgers and fries but the burgers are tasty.

ED'S CHOWDER HOUSE
Empire Hotel
44 W 63rd St (near Columbus Ave), 212-956-1288
https://www.facebook.com/EdsChowderHouse
CUISINE: Seafood
DRINKS: Full Bar
SERVING: Lunch & Dinner
PRICE RANGE: $$$
NEIGHBORHOOD: Upper West Side / Lincoln
Center
Located in the nearly 100-year-old Empire Hotel, this
sophisticated eatery that overlooks Lincoln Center is
seafood house serving up a menu of "sea shack
cuisine" which includes chowders, lobster (including
a damned good lobster roll that will make you think

you're on Cape Cod) and other fish selections. Here
you'll also find a raw bar. Menu favorites include:
Organic Atlantic salmon tartar and Chatham cod. A
lot of people don't know about this place or how good
it is. Draws a fashionable crowd.

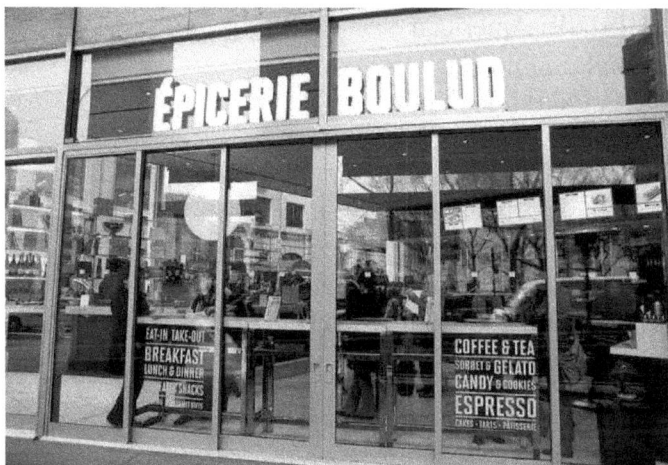

EPICERIE BOULUD
1900 Broadway (bet. 63th & 64th Sts), 212-595-9606
www.epiceriebloulud.com
CUISINE: Bakery, French
DRINKS: Beer & Wine Only
SERVING: Breakfast, Lunch & Dinner from 7 a.m.
PRICE RANGE: $$
NEIGHBORHOOD: Upper West Side
This modern gourmet café offers a menu that includes
everything from sandwiches and soups to cheeses and
charcuterie. Delicious desserts like pumpkin maple
pie. A great place to swing by before or after you
catch a performance at nearby Lincoln Center. A

perfect opportunity to pick up some of Daniel Boulud's great food to-go.

GEORGE KEELEY'S
485 Amsterdam Ave. (bet. 83rd & 84th Sts.): 212-873-0251
www.georgekeeley.com
CUISINE: American
DRINKS: Full Bar
SERVING: Late Night
PRICE RANGE: $$
NEIGHBORHOOD: Upper West Side
Popular sports bar with a friendly 30-something crowd. Great selection of beers on tap and free popcorn. Bar menu includes favorites like the epic Diablo burger and garlic fries. Plenty of flat screen TVs for watching sports. Theme nights. Friendly service.

GIN MILL
442 Amsterdam Ave (bet. 81st & 82nd Sts): 212-580-9080
www.nycbestbar.com

CUISINE: American
DRINKS: Full Bar
SERVING: Lunch & Dinner
PRICE RANGE: $$
NEIGHBORHOOD: Upper West Side
Popular sports bar featuring over 20 varieties of beer.
Menu includes favorites like burgers, wings, and
nachos. 28 large screen TVs show all the sports
games. Nightly specials and ½ price happy hour.

GOOD ENOUGH TO EAT
520 Columbus Ave (at 85th St), 212-496-0163
www.goodenoughtoeat.com
CUISINE: American, Comfort food
DRINKS: Full Bar
SERVING: Open daily for Breakfast, Lunch, Dinner
PRICE RANGE: $$$$
Here in this brick-walled dining room you can find
super good food. Known for executing American
comfort food with exacting standards, Chef Carrie
Levin offers up traditional favorites like meatloaf,
grilled steaks served with mashed potatoes, a great
Turkey Hash (with fresh roasted turkey, potatoes, red
bell peppers, carrots, celery, 2 poached eggs and
biscuits on the side). The turkey is always fresh here
because she serves a traditional Thanksgiving style
turkey dinner all year-round. Her excellent breakfast

selections are among the best in town (my favorite is
the BLT Omelette, with double-smoked bacon,
tomato and Gruyere: it's out of this world).

THE GRAND TIER RESTAURANT
METROPOLITAN OPERA HOUSE
30 Lincoln Center Plaza (at W 63rd St & Columbus
Ave), 212-799-3400

www.patinagroup.com/restaurant.php?restaurants_id=30
CUISINE: American
DRINKS: Full Bar
SERVING: Pre-theatre and intermission dining: Mon - Sat
PRICE RANGE: $$$$

THE GRANGE BAR & EATERY
1635 Amsterdam Ave (at W 141st St), 212-491-1635
www.thegrangebarnyc.com
CUISINE: American, Bar
DRINKS: Full Bar
SERVING: Lunch, Dinner, Open daily
PRICE RANGE: $$
Located in Hamilton Heights (named after Alexander Hamilton). The 16-ounce craft beer selection is listed on a blackboard hanging on an old brick wall behind the bar. The place is decorated with items that look like they came out of a barn or attic in an old house in the Carolinas, including the weathered wood. Farm-to-table produce is a big emphasis here, with a menu featuring items like lamb sliders, fish tacos, strawberry and arugula salad; spinach ravioli, a panko-crusted Portobello mushroom burger; an organic half-roasted organic chicken with 3-herb jus, fingerling potatoes. Very cozy atmosphere.

HARLEM SHAKE
100 W. 124th St, 212-222-8300
www.harlemshakenyc.com
CUISINE: American, Burgers
DRINKS: Beer & Wine
SERVING: Lunch & Dinner
PRICE RANGE: $$
NEIGHBORHOOD: Harlem
Great burger joint that serves a classic burger and a
Fatty Melt, which is two patties with cheese, pickles,
special sauce and onions served on thin grilled cheese
sandwiches instead of a bun. Here the food is made
from fresh quality ingredients. Try the signature
Harlem Shake.

JAKE'S DILEMMA
430 Amsterdam Ave. (bet. 80th & 81st Sts.): 212-580-
0556
www.nycbestbar.com
CUISINE: American
DRINKS: Full Bar
SERVING: Late Night
PRICE RANGE: $$

NEIGHBORHOOD: Upper West Side
Popular neighborhood sports bar offering over 50
different US beers and 14 beers on tap.
Drink specials and half price happy hour. Foosball
table and video games. Bar menu includes snacks like
nachos, chicken wings, tater tots, and mozzarella
sticks. Great prices and friendly crowd.

JEAN-GEORGES
Trump Hotel
1 Central Park West, New York: 212-299-3900
www.jean-georgesrestaurant.com/
CUISINE: French / American / Asian
DRINKS: Full bar
SERVING: Lunch, Dinner
NEIGHBORHOOD: Upper West Side
PRICE RANGE: $$$$; jackets required at dinner.
Flagship of **Jean-Georges Vongerichten**. I'd go with
the tasting menu either for lunch or dinner. They are
good values. (They have a 3-course tasting menu or
two 6-course menus.

LE BOITE EN BOIS
75 W 68th St (bet. Central Park West & Columbus
Ave), 212-874-2705
www.laboitenyc.com
CUISINE: French
DRINKS: Full Bar
SERVING: Lunch & Dinner
PRICE RANGE: $$$
NEIGHBORHOOD: Upper West Side
Longtime neighborhood favorite serving classic
French bistro fare. Favorites: Escargot and Veal

Scaloppini. Offers a pre-theater menu. 3 blocks from
Lincoln Center.

LION'S HEAD TAVERN
995 Amsterdam Ave. (109th St.): 212-866-1030
www.lionsheadnyc.com
CUISINE: Bar
DRINKS: Full Bar
SERVING: Bar Snacks
PRICE RANGE: $
NEIGHBORHOOD: Manhattan Valley
Very popular dive sports bar that has great drink
deals. Happy hour runs late. Eclectic mix of the
under-30 crowd. Bar menu of typical snacks like
wings and tater tots.

MAISON HARLEM
341 St Nicholas Ave (bet. 128th St & 127th St), 212-
222-9224
www.maisonharlem.com
CUISINE: French
DRINKS: Full Bar
SERVING: Breakfast, Lunch & Dinner
PRICE RANGE: $$
NEIGHBORHOOD: Harlem
French bistro serving classics. People gather in the
buzzy bar before going to the back of the room and
up a couple of steps into the dining room. Though the
leather booths in the back offer more privacy, I like to
grab a table at the front so I can look down at the
bustling bar scene. Favorites: Sea Bass and Merguez
de Barbes (grilled spicy homemade lamb sausages).
Great choice for breakfast.

MELBA'S
300 W 114th St (at Frederick Douglass Blvd), 212-864-7777
www.melbasrestaurant.com
CUISINE: Southern, American (Traditional), Soul Food
DRINKS: Full Bar
SERVING: Dinner nightly; brunch weekends
PRICE RANGE: $$
NEIGHBORHOOD: Harlem
Great comfort soul food restaurant with delicious dishes like BBQ turkey meatloaf served with candy yams and garlic mash potatoes. Popular spot for brunch with selections like the Eggnog Waffle. The salmon croquettes with grits is an excellent choice. Opened by Melba Wilson in 2005, she describes herself as Harlem "born, bred and buttered." (She previously worked at **Sylvia's**.

MINTON'S
206 W 118th St (near Adam Clayton Powell Blvd),
212-243-2222
www.mintonsharlem.com
CUISINE: American; Southern
DRINKS: Full Bar
SERVING: Dinner nightly from 5:30
PRICE RANGE: $$$
This jazz club offers an excellent menu to go with the
live jazz performed nightly. Low Country Seafood
platter gives you a tasting of blue crab fritter,
crawfish hushpuppy and fried oysters. She crab soup
with sherry is my absolute favorite—there's almost
nowhere you can get it in Manhattan. If you're feeling
particularly decadent, get the smothered lobster and
crab meat casserole. You'll need a crane to lift you
out of your chair. This is a great place to come if the
Cecil, located just next door, is really busy.

MOMOFUKU MILK BAR
561 Columbus Ave (at 87th St), 646-692-4154
www.milkbarstore.com
CUISINE: Bakery, Ice Cream & Frozen Yogurt
DRINKS: No Booze
SERVING: Desserts
PRICE RANGE: $$
NEIGHBORHOOD: Upper West Side
Super cool place to stop in for a treat. Very creative
things going on in here. This dessert specialty shop
offers a variety of freshly baked cookies, cakes and
pies. Popular items include the Confetti Cookie and
Cornflake Baking Mixes. Specialty favorites include
Cereal Milk (milk that tastes like it was poured from a

bowl of cereal). Small lunch menu available. Novelty items for sale like T-shirts, bags, and cookbooks.

NICE MATIN
201 W 79th St (at Amsterdam Ave): 212-873 6423
www.nicematinnyc.com
CUISINE: French
DRINKS: full bar
SERVING: breakfast (from 7 a.m.), lunch, dinner
NEIGHBORHOOD: Upper West Side
PRICE RANGE: $$
This neighborhood place, good for any meal of the day, is inspired by the food from the south of France, though it's mostly American. It's reasonable, has a superior wine list with great bargains, and the food is as good as anywhere else from a great chef, **Andy D'Amico.** You'd be a regular here if you lived around the corner.

NOUGATINE AT JEAN-GEORGES
1 Central Park West (at 59th St & Columbus Circle), 212-299-3900
www.jean-georgesrestaurant.com/nougatine-and-terrace-at-jean-georges

143

CUISINE: French
DRINKS: Full Bar
SERVING: Breakfast, Lunch, Dinner daily
PRICE RANGE: $$$
You get a picture perfect view of Central Park at street level through the floor-to-ceiling windows at this little sleek and modern island of tranquility at Jean-Georges. The outdoor Terrace is perfect when the weather's good. Both Nougatine and the Terrace offer less formal cuisine than the Jean-Georges, but it's just as good in a less fussy atmosphere. Foie fras brule, peekytoe crab cake; rigatoni with meatballs; roasted Dover sole.

OXBOW TAVERN
240 Columbus Ave (71st St), 212-490-4075
www.oxbowtavern.com
CUISINE: French/American
DRINKS: Full Bar
SERVING: Dinner
PRICE RANGE: $$$
NEIGHBORHOOD: Upper West Side
Cozy, romantic French eatery. Nice menu. Favorites: Pan Roasted East Coast Halibut and Coq Au Vin.

PASHA RESTAURANT
70 W 71st St (between W Central park & Columbus Ave), 212-579-8751 www.pashanewyork.com
CUISINE: Turkish
DRINKS: Full Bar
SERVING: Lunch & Dinner
PRICE RANGE: $$
NEIGHBORHOOD: Upper West Side

A quaint restaurant with a comfortable ambiance that serves a regal menu of authentic Turkish cuisine. Menu favorites include: Octopus salad and Charcoal Grilled lamb medallions. Interesting wine list. Excellent service.

PER SE
Time Warner Center
10 Columbus Circle, New York: 212-823-9335
www.perseny.com
CUISINE: French
DRINKS: Full bar
SERVING: Dinner nightly, Lunch (Fri – Sun)
NEIGHBORHOOD: Midtown West
PRICE RANGE: $$$$+

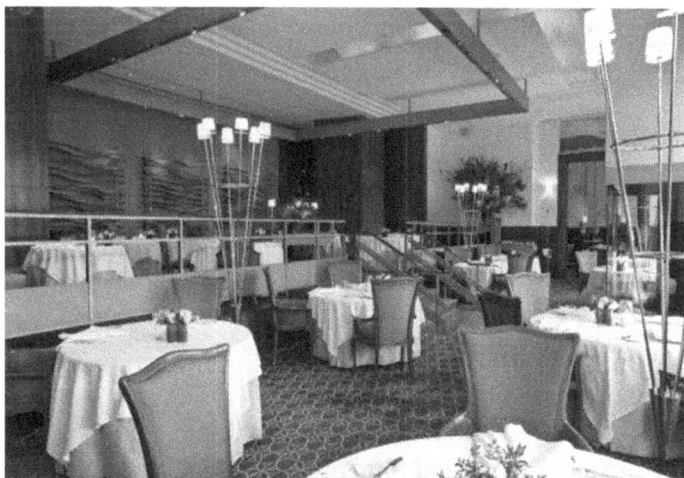

Famed Chef **Thomas Keller** is behind this place, considered to be one of the best restaurants in the world. The menu is fixed, so you can expect a dizzying array of delectable masterpieces. (When you finish, the waiter will bring by a box containing handmade chocolates—they'll explain to you what the filling is in each one—a nice touch to wrap up a memorable evening.)

PIER i CAFÉ
500 W 70th St (at Riverside Blvd), 212-362-4450
www.piericafe.com
CUISINE: American
DRINKS: Full Bar
SERVING: Lunch, Dinner, Open daily
PRICE RANGE: $$
Way up here tucked beneath the elevated West Side Highway by Riverside Park you'll find a little spot that you'd think would never make sense given where it's located. But the luscious burgers served here complement the extraordinary sunsets visible from this unique perspective.

PROHIBITION
503 Columbus Ave. (bet. 84th & 85th Sts): 212-579-3100
www.prohibition.net
CUISINE: Seafood
DRINKS: Beer & Wine Only
SERVING: Lunch & Dinner
PRICE RANGE: $$
NEIGHBORHOOD: Upper West Side
This upscale bar and lounge features live music nightly covering a variety of musical genres from groovy funk to jazz. Cool décor and funky atmosphere, this popular bar serves classic cocktails from the Prohibition era and a variety of specially

drinks. Menu features New American favorites like the sombrero salad with spinach, shrimp, corn, and jalapeno cheese. No cover charge.

RED ROOSTER
310 Lenox Ave, 212-792-9001
www.redroosterharlem.com
CUISINE: Soul Food, American
DRINKS: Full Bar
SERVING: Lunch & Dinner
PRICE RANGE: $$$
NEIGHBORHOOD: Harlem
This attractive eatery serves comfort food that reflects the diverse traditions of the neighborhood. Menu

favorites include: Chicken and waffles; Catfish; fried green tomatoes served with iceberg lettuce, bacon and buttermilk dressing; dirty rice and shrimp. This place attracts a very New York mix of the trendy as well as tourists. The chef, Marcus Samuelsson, was born in

Ethiopia, but he was raised in Sweden, so he's got some interesting twists on almost every dish. (He worked at the highly acclaimed Aquavit.) For dessert order the donuts or the dark chocolate cheesecake. Impressive wine list.

SARABETH'S WEST
423 Amsterdam Ave (between 80th & 81st Sts), 212-496-6280
www.sarabethsrestaurants.com/upper-west-side
CUISINE: American
DRINKS: Full Bar
SERVING: Breakfast, Lunch & Dinner
PRICE RANGE: $$
NEIGHBORHOOD: Upper West Side
A popular spot famous for its brunch, this comfortable eatery has been serving up home-style cooking for nearly 30 years. Menu favorites include: Almond crusted French toast and the Pumpkin Waffle. Expect a wait if you go on the weekend.

SHALEL LOUNGE
65 W. 70th St., downstairs (bet. Columbus Ave. & CPW): 212-873-2300
https://www.facebook.com/pages/Shalel-Lounge/115323131854627
CUISINE: Moroccan
DRINKS: Full Bar
SERVING: Late Night
PRICE RANGE: $$
NEIGHBORHOOD: Upper West Side
A Moroccan-inspired lounge located downstairs giving it a cavernous feel. Romantic atmosphere is

suitable for a date. Impressive wine selection. Menu favorites include: Moroccan lamb in phyllo dough. Private rooms available.

THE SMITH
1900 Broadway (at W 63rd St), 212-496-5700
www.thesmithnyc.com
CUISINE: American
DRINKS: Full Bar
SERVING: Breakfast, Lunch, Dinner, Open Daily,
PRICE RANGE: $$
While the 50-foot-long zinc-topped bar is a big attraction, even bigger is the swell crowd that pushes into this place after work and before the theatre.

SYLVIA'S

328 Malcolm X Blvd, 212-996-0660
www.sylviasrestaurant.com
CUISINE: Soul Food, Seafood
DRINKS: Full Bar
SERVING: Lunch & Dinner
PRICE RANGE: $$
NEIGHBORHOOD: Harlem

Named after Sylvia Woods, the "Queen of Soulfood,"
Sylvia's certainly lives up to the reputation. Great
selection of soul food and good home cooking with
delicious sides like Candied yams and Mac & Cheese.
Dine at the counter or in the dining area. Very
popular Sunday brunch spot but arrive early if you
want a table. Though Woods died in 2012, the place
is as popular as ever. The Rev. Al Sharpton said he'd

dined here with everybody from President Obama to
Caroline Kennedy.

TAVERN ON THE GREEN
67 Central Park W (67th St), 212-877-8684
www.tavernonthegreen.com
CUISINE: Steakhouse/American (New)
DRINKS: Full Bar
SERVING: Lunch & Dinner, Weekend brunch
PRICE RANGE: $$$
NEIGHBORHOOD: Central Park

Restored Central Park icon serving a menu of
American fare with 700 seats sprawling out over
several rooms. No one who's ever been here in the
old days will ever forget it. One night I particularly
remember was in the Crystal Room on a snowy
night—the image of the snow gently falling outside
with hundreds of white twinkling lights in the trees
was spellbinding. That was then—this is now. Menu
picks: Beef Carpaccio and Salmon & Scallops.
Popular spot for brunch, though the food is decidedly

unspectacular. The setting, however, very much is. Nice cocktails and wine selection. Reservations recommended. Great view of the park.

TESSA
349 Amsterdam Ave (W 77th St), 212-390-1974
http://tessanyc.com/
CUISINE: American, French, Italian
DRINKS: Full Bar
SERVING: Lunch, Dinner & Late Night
PRICE RANGE: $$$
The new industrial styled eatery run by Chef Cedric Tovar, formerly of Peacock Alley, serves French-Mediterranean cuisine.

VIAND
2130 Broadway (at 75th St) 212-877-2888
www.viandcafenyc.com
CUISINE: Coffeeshop
DRINKS: Full Bar
SERVING: Lunch & Dinner
PRICE RANGE: $$
NEIGHBORHOOD: Upper West Side
A small diner with a counter and small two-person booths serves typical diner cuisine, but of very high quality and cheap prices. Menu favorites include the create-your-own omelette, the super deli sandwiches (the hot open-faced roast beef sandwich is great) and burgers. Crowded. No bathroom.

Upper West Side Budget Spots

AFRICA KINE
2267 7th Ave (bet. W 133rd St & w 134th St), 212-666-9400
www.africakine.com
CUISINE: Fast Food
DRINKS: No Booze
SERVING: Lunch & Dinner
PRICE RANGE: $$
NEIGHBORHOOD: Harlem
Small eatery serving a varied menu of traditional African comfort fare. Favorites: Lamb mate; thiebou guinaar; Dibi chicken and Lamb with plantains. There are too many places serving this kind of food in America. Enjoy this on your visit. Women cook during lunch, while at dinner the men come in for their shift.

EL MALECON
764 Amsterdam Ave. (bet. 97th St. & 98th St.), 212-864-5648
www.maleconrestaurants.com
CUISINE: Latin American, Caribbean; Dominican
DRINKS: Beer & Wine
SERVING: Lunch, Dinner
NEIGHBORHOOD: Upper West Side / Manhattan Valley

PRICE RANGE: $
Good cheap Latin food. Especially good rotisserie
chicken. Mofongo (smashed plantains) with shrimp is
a winner.

GRAY'S PAPAYA
2090 Broadway (W 72nd St), 212-799-0243
CUISINE: Hot Dogs/Smoothies
DRINKS: No Booze
SERVING: 24 hours
PRICE RANGE: $
NEIGHBORHOOD: Upper West Side
This popular chain of all-hot dog stands has been
serving NYC forever. Grab a hot dog and a papaya
beverage.

THE HANDPULLED NOODLE
3600 Broadway (W 148th St), 917-262-0213
www.thehandpullednoodle.com
CUISINE: China (northwest area)
DRINKS: No Booze
SERVING: Lunch & Dinner
PRICE RANGE: $
NEIGHBORHOOD: Harlem / Hamilton Heights

Funky storefront eatery offering a variety menu of noodles and dumplings. Favorites: Dapanji (a beautifully fragrant stew anchored by chicken on the bone and lots of cardamom); Drunken noodles and Mama's Jumbo Lamb & Carrot Dumplings. Delivery available.

HILL COUNTRY CHICKEN
1123 Broadway, New York: 212-257-6446
www.hillcountrychicken.com/
CUISINE: Southern
DRINKS: Beer & Wine
SERVING: Breakfast, Lunch, Dinner
NEIGHBORHOOD: Midtown South
PRICE RANGE: $$
You're coming here for fried chicken, period. Helpful staff, busy and exciting atmosphere in a fun-filled place. Bright and cheerful, with yellow being a prominent color. Cheesy mashed potatoes and don't overlook the pies.

LA SAVANE
239 W 116th St (bet. 7th Ave & St Nicholas Ave), 646-490-4644
http://www.lasavanerestaurant.com/
CUISINE: West African / Ivorian / Pan African
DRINKS: No Booze
SERVING: Lunch & Dinner
PRICE RANGE: $
NEIGHBORHOOD: Harlem
Simple eatery serving authentic West African cuisine. There's a beautiful mural painted on the all depicting villagers near their thatched roof houses tending to a

giant cauldron in the middle of the village. Nothing fancy. They don't even have knives. On a weekend night you'll see people from different countries speaking French and English. Unlike you, they won't look at the menu when they order. Favorites: Lamb shanks exceeding tasty; Guinea fowl cut into pieces and deep fried; grilled lamb with oil and sautéed onions slathered over it. Be careful when you use the hot sauce here—it's eye-watering.

LOLO'S SEAFOOD SHACK
303 W 116th St (Frederick Douglass Blvd), 646-649-3356
www.lolosseafoodshack.com
CUISINE: Seafood/Sandwiches
DRINKS: Beer & Wine
SERVING: Lunch & Dinner
PRICE RANGE: $
NEIGHBORHOOD: Harlem

Small counter-order eatery serving Caribbean-inspired fare, seafood, and sandwiches. There is a small dining room in the back of the house. (A "lolo" is an outdoor BBQ pit or roadside stand found in the West Indies.) Picks: Conch Fritters using rice flour that lightens them up a bit; Smelts deep-fried & served over plantains; Plantain Johnny Cake sandwich (perfect). Outdoor seating in the decked over yard out in the rear, weather permitting.

SAFARI
219 W 116th St, (bet. 7th Ave & St Nicholas Ave), 646-964-4252
www.safariharlem.com
CUISINE: East African / Somali
DRINKS: No Booze; good selection of juices
SERVING: Lunch & Dinner
PRICE RANGE: $$
NEIGHBORHOOD: Harlem
Laid-back café serving Somali and East African fare. This part of town houses the largest concentration of West African immigrants, so there are lots of places to eat that offer most Americans food they've never tasted before. But since Somalia is across the African continent, the food here isn't reflective of the West African cuisines you'll find in this neighborhood. Known as the first and only Somali eatery in NYC. Favorites: Beef & chicken sambusa and Chicken suqaar (spicy chicken stew with basmati rice). Chicken dishes are the best, but the goat (roasted for 6 hours) is excellent. Teas and homemade juice.

TOM'S RESTAURANT
2880 Broadway (bet. 112th St & 111th St), 212-864-6137
www.tomsrestaurant.net
CUISINE: Diner
DRINKS: No Booze
SERVING: Breakfast, Lunch & Dinner: open 24 hours Thurs-Sat
PRICE RANGE: $
NEIGHBORHOOD: Morningside Heights
Local coffee shop known for its cameo on TV show "Seinfeld." Typical diner food. Burgers, sandwiches, Chicken parm. Photos from the iconic TV show adorn the walls. Cash only.

INDEX

DID YOU FIND AN INTERESTING PLACE?

If you discover a place you think I should check out on my next visit, drop me a line, will you? I'll mention your name if I end up listing it.

andrewdelaplaine@mac.com

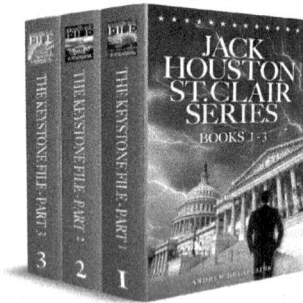

WANT 3 FREE THRILLERS?

Why, of course you do!

If you like these writers--

Vince Flynn, Brad Thor, Tom Clancy, James Patterson, David Baldacci, John Grisham, Brad Meltzer, Daniel Silva, Don DeLillo

www.ingramcontent.com/pod-product-compliance
Lightning Source LLC
Chambersburg PA
CBHW071442090426
42737CB00011B/1751